SALES ECONOMICS:
THE SCIENCE OF SELLING

Jordan,
I expect huge success for you.
Trust the science. It will take you to
the stars... and beyond.
You are special.
Sincerely,
Rich   January 2020

SALES ECONOMICS:
The Science of Selling

RICK DAVIS

Hard Knock Press

To book Rick as a speaker for your next event or to learn more about sales and sales management training programs for your company, visit **www.buildingleaders.com**.

First published by Hard Knock Press, September 2019

Cover design by Lynda Van Duerm
Interior layout by Vickie Swisher, Studio 20|20

ISBN: 978-0-9847114-4-4 (hc)
ISBN: 978-0-9847114-3-7 (pb)
Library of Congress Control Number: 2019911679

TO MY MOM

Contents

Preface: About the Cover

You might wonder why that funny diagram is on the front cover. It is a fractal, a repeating pattern that continues across different scales. Each extension of the pattern is identical and produces a subsequent repetition of the pattern.

Even if you don't know it, you've seen fractals many times in nature. They occur in trees when one branch sprouts two smaller branches on one side and three on another. The leaf patterns of the same tree follow by producing two veins on one side and three on the other. The pattern is repeated off the smaller veins. And so forth.

Fractals are seen in snowflakes, mollusks, crystals, plants, and other forms of nature. Fractals have been used to design computer chips, create valuable mathematical predictions, produce medical diagnoses, and allow cell phone antennae to connect on multiple frequencies.

Sales Economics leverages the concept of fractals to create predictability specific to the process of selling. The cover art illustrates one fractal form that can be proactively designed when a salesperson engages in the process of sales advocacy, a concept to be defined in the book. Other fractals produce repeated patterns of sales call development, calendar management, relationship development, and ways to sell effectively, build relationships, and achieve long-term sales goals with repeatable success.

Acknowledgements

Writing a book is hard. Writers sit in the vacuum of their heads and type paragraphs that become sentences before diminishing into a jumble of words and letters that feel as if they make no sense at all. There are initial drafts, minor edits, massive painful deletion of pages, debates about content development, and ultimately the invaluable support of people that enable the writer to become an author. It certainly does not happen alone...

Most certainly it does not happen without Ellice Herman, my close friend and the Director of Important Stuff at Building Leaders, Inc. She kept our business running and helped me endure emotional ups and downs while convincing me to soldier on when the project became overwhelming. She is a source of inspiration and a truly gifted editor. Her knowledge of sales is extensive and the lively dialogues we shared about sales theory make the work richer for her contributions. Her heart and soul are in every page of this book.

Shelley Chung delivered the editing expertise necessary to make the words flow. She helped organize concepts and provided supportive feedback above and beyond the call of duty. She inspired me to stick with the project while offering an education in book editing that has made me a more confident writer in the process. If and when I get the energy to take on a project like this again, she will hopefully participate on the journey.

Mark Hansen is a sales powerhouse and professional associate on whom I have relied for years to vet sales concepts and practices. He provided vital suggestions that significantly affected the presentation of theories. I thank him for reading the entire manuscript and taking the time to sit with me and pore through the concepts while delivering abundant praise and the tactful, constructive feedback necessary to polish the work.

Rick Schumacher, editor of LBM Journal, set me on the course with the simple words "it's time to write a new book." Thank you, my friend. Big contributions come in surprisingly small packages.

Andy Schwegel, a longtime friend and thoughtful business leader, simply said, "You should write a book on business-to-business sales." It is amazing how one little sentence can crystalize the presentation of many thousands of words.

A book is more than words, but also a work of art. The artists I work with, Lynda Van Duerm who always makes my graphic depictions of theories look better, and Vickie Swisher, the wonderful artist who laid out the pages, are godsends.

Other wonderful guideposts in my journey included Suzanne Murray, Louis Segovia, Jane Dillingham, Beth Naulty, and the Vegas crew. As always, I would be remiss if I didn't recognize Bob Eckert and Tom Latourette who helped me launch in the first place.

…And Meg. You are the most grounded person I know and help me every day in ways too immeasurable to reckon.

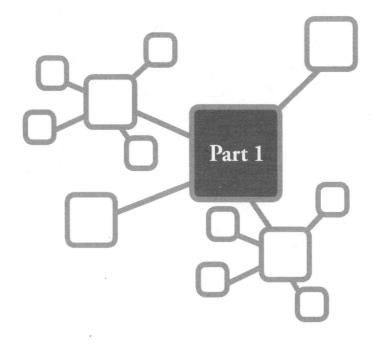

Part 1

FOUNDATIONAL
CONCEPTS

1

Microsales,
Macrosales, and
Behavioral Sales Bias

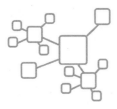

From Opinions to Sales Science

Sales Economics provides a new discipline to reveal correlations between sales performance and outcomes—i.e., *sales science*. The goal is to build legitimate expertise in a profession in which no unanimous assessment of performance excellence has been established. Unlike other professional disciplines, there are no credentials to establish sales authority. Doctors, accountants, lawyers, architects, financial planners, and a multitude of other professions require educational and certification credentials. Sales economics might not provide official credentials, but will provide credibility through expertise.

Sales Economics is primarily, but not exclusively, for salespeople in business-to-business roles although any serious student of the profession will gain significantly from the concepts. The focus is business-to-business simply because the process of selling to business entities is different than selling to a consumer. The buyer is a professional purchasing agent trained in negotiations. The sales cycle is longer. The purchaser is not usually buying a product for consumption, but instead as a tool to create profit. Still, *any* salesperson who consumes the ideas in this book will gain the power to create performance measurements and evaluate them objectively.

Sales Economics strives to reduce the reliance on armchair theories and opinions that are not proven with any significant degree of objectivity. Successful salespeople as well as those who have failed are experts at giving sales advice. Executives who did not get the results they wanted from salespeople are experts at criticizing sales failure. There are a lot of opinions from people willing to give advice about their versions of the correct sales process. It's easy to tell people what to do in the absence of science. Sales economics eliminates guesswork.

I became a salesperson because it was my best chance to make money. I deluded myself briefly into believing it would be easy. I fancied myself a good conversationalist and was a fearless speaker standing before a large audience. The thing is, however, selling is not just talking and it's not easy. It's complicated.

Thousands of salespeople are placed in the role of sales with little more training than a pat on the back and a wish for good luck...like I was. No credentials. No training. Lots of hope. Over a career spanning decades, I have yet to meet anyone whose major was "sales sciences" in college. While studying economics, I don't recall a single class that my university offered on the subject of selling. I became a salesman because, after college, I didn't feel qualified to do much else.

The outcome was predictable. My initiation to the profession was a roller coaster of terror, depression, and very brief periods of thrill. Like lots of salespeople, I was scared most of the time. I don't share my story to write a memoir, but instead to openly admit the fears and emotional challenges that a lot of people endure in a very difficult profession.

Selling is the profession of fear. People hold you accountable for results without providing the means to achieve them. It's easy to quantify sales outcomes, not so easy to quantify performance. Therefore, performance evaluation comes down to a matter of opinions of so-called experts.

I was an economics student long before I became a student of selling. I fell into the profession of selling by accident like a lot of other salespeople and now, years later, base my credentials on a multitude of career experiences. I have traversed a journey during which I have been employed as a salesman, manager, and executive. I have since become a consultant to hundreds of sales organizations and learned lessons based on decades of observations, measurements, and conversations with thousands of salespeople. The result is the discovery of links between sales behaviors, measurement of performance data, and future outcomes. In short, I make observations and seek causality. That's what economists do.

We make observations about data and activity while correlating outcomes. We try to make predictions based on theory, testing, mathematical formulas, and other means. It's a fun social science because it leverages ideas in mathematics, marketing, philosophy, psychology, scientific experimentation, and more. It's a challenging discipline because the science is often inexact, which in no way should stop the exploration.

The simple objective is to remove as much opinion as possible from the equations and define the facts that predict future results. If they can't be defined unequivocally, at least we should establish a process of improvement that allows *you* to define them better. That being said, I think you're in for a treat. There is some fun stuff in here that any reader might enjoy as we answer simple yet vital questions to provide scientific expertise about the profession of selling.

A Game Plan on Offense

Why do three salespeople achieve very different levels of success while working in identical roles? The salesperson at one desk of the car dealership sells thirty cars per month while a long-time industry veteran at another desk sells less than a dozen, and a third fails to make it in the business after a few months. The easy answer is to say that one salesperson is simply "better" than another. But why? What are they doing differently? Can we measure those differences statistically? Can we teach underperforming salespeople to improve or is success purely a function of desire? In other words, are salespeople born or made? These questions, and more, bother me. They have become my life work and provided the genesis of this book.

In nearly every aspect of business, leaders and managers can point to data that determine future outcomes and links to profitability, particularly in finance and operational management. The cost of labor and overtime provides planning insights to control variable expenses. The cost of equipment enables manufacturers to determine levels of production necessity. The cost of money provides the insights necessary to calculate required sales volume and profit margin. Other expense measurements enable managers to predict the future costs of doing business and ways to control the bottom line.

Oops! Wait. Let's go back. Did you catch those two little items in the middle of the paragraph that said executives and owners know how to "calculate required sales volume and profit margin" to achieve proper return on investment? There is a problem in there. They know *what* results are needed, but many do not *how* to produce them. They know how to manage costs and establish topline sales requirements, but no plan to comfortably *predict* those sales outcomes. There is a great plan on *defense* for controlling and managing expenses and assets, but not so much on *offense*. Crazy if you think about it, right?

Imagine an offensive football coordinator sending the team onto the field without a playbook. Instead, because he has no clue himself what needs to be done, he huddles up his players and says, "Just put those points on the board, boys. You can do it!" Chances for success in this scenario are unlikely and, if even achieved, purely accidental. As ridiculous as it sounds, this is exactly what happens in the corporate world every day. Revenue predictions are a guess as evidenced by the financial reports rife with news of companies that fall short of sales and earnings projections. The quality of sales performance is a hunch as evidenced by managers throughout the world who lament frustrations about their underachieving salespeople; if the managers had a plan, they would lament less and coach more.

Selling, for any business, is offense. The points on the board, in the form of sales, must be greater than the points allowed. Profitability is the difference between the topline revenue and the sum of expenses. Revenue must be greater, or the organization loses. The vital questions, therefore, remain unanswered. How does a business organization put points on the board? How will they achieve *predictable* sales volume and margins?

Sales Economics answers questions about sales predictability and provides a game plan for offense. Why do people buy? How can organizations and individuals create predictable sales outcomes? What are the metrics that predict future sales success? Why do salespeople unnecessarily sacrifice profits during casual negotiations? Why do some companies selling identical products have such different profit margins? What current fallacies about sales measurement hamper success? Can you assess the quality and value of a sales call objectively? Are salespeople born or made? In short, there are a lot of good questions to answer that help salespeople achieve success on purpose.

Traditional Economics to Sales Economics

Traditional economics is the study of assumptions, outcomes, and future market predictability. Economic theories strive to illustrate how societies, organizations, and individuals allocate scarce resources at their disposal. The discipline has been divided into two conventional categories—microeconomics and macroeconomics. Microeconomics describes ways in which organizations manage resources, price goods, and maximize profits. Macroeconomics analyzes societies and the global economy by observing the effects of government fiscal policies, implications of money supplies in various countries, interest rate decisions, and other large-picture issues.

As noted earlier, economics is part mathematics and part social science where predictions are based on assumptions about human behavior. These traditional economic assumptions are being challenged to develop better conclusions through the study of a relatively new branch in economics called behavioral economics. Beginning in the 1970s, economists Amos Tversky, Daniel Kahneman, and Richard Thaler pioneered concepts in behavioral economics for which Thaler and Kahneman separately won Nobel Prizes for their work, the latter of which would have likely been shared with Tversky had he not passed away (you have to be alive to earn a Nobel Prize).

Traditional economic theory presumes that human beings are rational and possess equal access to complete market information thus producing consistent, predictable decision-making. Of course this is folly. The trio of behavioral economists, and others, have cited multitudes of examples where bias, passion, fear, and other emotions affect decisions.

Thaler writes that economists have treated human beings as if they are a homogenous buying group all behaving identically as rational, cold-blooded decision-makers that always optimize outcomes logically. Human beings are, of course, emotional and psychological. They are hardly robotic, logical decision-makers. The field of behavioral economics seeks to discover how we can better predict the responses in varying buying situations of something very unpredictable— i.e., human beings.

If ever there were a situation in which we could expect cold-blooded, rational decision-making, it would be where so-called investment "experts," with equal information access, would come to similar, if not identical, conclusions. But they don't. In a January 15, 2013, issue of *Forbes* magazine, Frederick Allen reported that a housecat named Orlando did a better job of picking stocks than three professional brokers.

In *Thinking Fast and Slow*, Kahneman asserts that the stock market industry of professional investors appears to be "built largely on an *illusion of skill*." Several professional investors were analyzed, including a mutual fund manager who invested tens of millions of dollars for no other reason than he had been impressed by the cars he saw at an auto show. Kahneman cites a paper by Brad Barber and Terrance Odean titled "Trading Is Hazardous to Your Wealth," which proved that overly active traders achieved the worst results. Kahneman later concluded that it would have been a wiser investment strategy to do nothing rather than act on every investment idea that popped into their minds.

The supposedly smartest investors in the world were expected to do better than the average, yet failed, and led Kahneman to a surprisingly rational conclusion. Apparently, the investment professionals—supposedly cold-blooded analyzers of stock value—are as irrational as a housecat. These anecdotal stories in behavioral economics illustrate the inconsistency of decision-making among buyers, even the most expectedly rational ones!

Humans are far from rational and usually make decisions with incomplete information. They hardly behave with predictable consistency. Not surprisingly, neither do *salespeople* because they are humans, too! This takes us from the study of economics to a narrower field of study, specifically *sales* economics.

Sellers Are Human, Too

Admittedly it would be hubris to believe I could add to the concepts in buyer rationale that hasn't been covered by three geniuses and other academics in the field of behavioral economics, nor is that my intent. *Sales Economics* is not the endeavor to understand how buyers think, although you will be exposed to some concepts in the decision-making process of buyers. It is the study of sales performance and the mindset of *sellers*.

Sellers are not robotic, rational beings either. They have fears, dreams, beliefs, and experiences that significantly impact their performance and decision-making. The inconsistent performance of companies and the unpredictable behaviors of hundreds of salespeople proves that sales bias and beliefs dramatically affects outcomes. One salesperson confidently sees an opportunity to hold firm on price while another in the identical situation fears a lost sale. The difference is not the situation, but rather the subjective bias and beliefs of each salesperson.

Sales Economics illustrates how the bias and beliefs of salespeople influence outcomes, but would be incomplete without delving into a mathematical analysis of the sales process and the larger, long-term picture of sales accomplishment. The study of economics is broken down into the three major categories that include microeconomics, macroeconomics, and behavioral economics. I have broken the study of *Sales Economics* into three categories as well: *behavioral sales economics, microsales economics,* and *macrosales economics.*

Behavioral sales economics reveals ideas about performance and emotional bias while providing links between sales actions and outcomes. The emphasis, while tangentially addressing buyer bias and motivations, will emphasize how to assess performance bias of salespeople and define a process for objective self-observation and constant personal growth. Behavioral sales economics will illustrate how to recognize recurring sales situations to plan strategies and test tactics objectively. The outcome of the study in behavioral sales economics is a formula for process improvement directly under the control of the salesperson. No gimmicks or second-guessing, but instead a process to measure the effectiveness of behaviors.

Microsales economics will measure the interactions between sellers and buyers by analyzing the quality of sales meetings with mathematical objectivity. Microsales economics includes the traditional lessons in sales interactions including skills of prospecting, questioning, presentations, handling objections, and more. Whereas typical sales training theory invents a process for salespeople to follow, microsales theory instead measures and reveals the process.

At the macrosales level you will discover how to measure the larger picture of sales performance. Macrosales provides the mathematics and tools for individual long-term sales achievement that translate into larger organizational success. Formulas will provide predictions to plan sales campaigns and achieve long-term goals with high degrees of predictability.

Sales Economics is sprinkled with a variety of common-sense ideas, personal experiences, case studies, and doses of mathematical formulas that have been tested to work. Admittedly, you will have to discover what works for you because the truth about selling is that the process is highly situational.

Selling airplanes is different than selling shoes because an airplane requires a longer consultative process with highly educated engineers versus the simpler selection of shoes for a walk-in consumer. Two people selling an identical product will face very different sales challenges. For example, the representative of a car manufacturer promotes a long-term campaign of events, marketing, and inventory plans to a dealer; the dealer salesperson, on the other hand, faces the pressure of creating transactional success on a daily basis.

In the business-to-business realm, sales roles and consultative challenges differ. The salesperson for a medical prosthetic company works in a hospital environment with doctors to understand the mechanics of human engineering and very specific product applications. A paper towel salesperson would not focus at all on product applications during a sales interaction with the grocery store purchasing agent. The quicker-picker-upper ads have pretty much taught consumers for years what they need to know; the paper towel salesperson instead provides consultation for retail merchandising.

Some salespeople must expect long selling cycles while others expect to close deals in a matter of hours or minutes. Some salespeople deal with multiple decision-makers while others deal with a single person making a final decision. The roles and processes vary slightly and greatly, depending on products, industries, client demographics, and more. The good news is that you can make it all very simple with a scientific approach. No matter what you sell, you will gain methods to measure and improve your performance in pursuit of predictable future results...*on purpose.*

2

Sales Success
on Purpose

Accidental Success

It surprises people to hear that I was once a professional golfer, which is quite a feat when your average score per hole is a bogey. Yet I managed it by working for a manufacturer of windows. My territory included four states through which I diligently drove on a dedicated route of service calls. Samples and customer files were tucked neatly in the trunk of my car *after* first ensuring that my golf clubs had their own home, which means I golfed a lot and sold ineffectively. I was getting paid and, therefore, a professional golfer of sorts.

To be fair, it was my first job and I received no sales training. My manager never once coached me in one-on-one dialogues or rode in my territory to observe my performance. If that were not enough baggage for a young man entering a challenging profession, the window company was experiencing product defects at the rate of 100%. Every product produced over a three-year period needed replacement and, not surprisingly, the company was being sued while verging on bankruptcy. My days and weeks consisted of driving between cities to get yelled at by customers, which led to bouts of anxiety and depression. The company eventually folded and I now consider myself fortunate for the experience.

Had I worked for a successful company, I might never have faced the truth of my incompetence because, despite the catastrophic manufacturing defects and tarnished brand image, orders were coming in that had nothing to do with me. I processed almost none of them because they were sent directly to the home office. I golfed, customers yelled, and orders flowed. I had ample reasons to be ignorant of my ineptitude, most notably an ineffective manager who told me I was doing a good job!

He never once observed my performance and instead relied on sales call reports that were creative writing masterpieces. For example, one prospect kicked me out of his office for not having an appointment and said, "I'll be delighted to talk to you in a few weeks if you make an appointment, but you can't barge in unannounced. Please leave." My call report said, "Met great new prospect. 'Delighted' to learn more about our product and wants to schedule follow-up meeting." It wasn't exactly a lie, so who was I to know that I was terrible at my job? The manager thought I was doing well simply because sales in my territory were rising. I was selling by accident.

Transactional Dependability

It turns out that many salespeople enjoy the fortunate circumstance of a dependable stream of inbound orders. I define this economic sales condition as *high transactional dependability*, which occurs when a salesperson can *depend on habitual repeat purchases based on a formal commitment from the buyer*. Orders arrive from customers who are the product resellers whether the salesperson is present or not, competent or not. The pressure to create transactions is low.

The pressure, or sales "heat," as I like to call it, escalates the closer the salesperson is to the consumer. In my case, my direct customer was the window dealer who sold to a builder who in turn sold to the consumer. I was three levels removed from the final buyer. In some supply chain scenarios there is another level of regional distribution between the dealer and manufacturer that leaves the sales rep four levels removed. In other industries, automobiles for example, the manufacturer sales rep is two levels removed, where the dealer is the only buffer between the manufacturer rep and the consumer, although this isn't the point.

The key point is that some salespeople enjoy a high level of transactional security that others do not. The manufacturer representative for the car dealer has a high degree of security due to the virtual guarantee transactions will keep flowing. The salesperson's customer is a car dealer contractually obligated to the supplier, deeply committed to inventory, and aligned so tightly with the brand that shifting alliances is extremely problematic. High transactional dependability enables salespeople to ignore performance feedback and improvement because, after all, a secure flow of transactions creates comfort and a steady income.

I was one of those salespeople who enjoyed the luxury, like many manufacturer sales reps, of transferring the sales heat. I relied on the dealer to order products because the dealer salespeople kept generating transactions with builders. The dealer salesperson, on the other hand, lives every day with the anxiety of generating daily transactions with new customers. This is a condition we can define with the economic term *low transactional dependability*, which is occurs *when the salesperson must repeatedly influence decisions to different buying audiences.*

The Rising Heat of Transactional Necessity

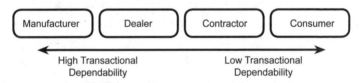

Figure 2.1: The closer the sales representative works with the last buyer in the supply chain, the greater the transactional "heat" in the form of *low* transactional dependability. The further a sales representative gets from the end user, the *higher* the degree of transactional dependability.

Figure 2.1 illustrates, for the construction supply chain, varying degrees of transactional dependability. The manufacturer sales rep has the highest degree of transactional dependability; the salesperson directly interacting with the consumer has the lowest degree of transactional dependability; the dealer reselling the manufactured goods is a degree somewhere in between, all of which we can measure!

Measuring Dependability

Transactional dependability is the *measurement of inbound sales from new buyers and volume retention from repeat customer purchases that can be produced with little or no intervention by the salesperson.* For example, a car manufacturer typically enjoys relationships with their dealers that endure years. Most sales representatives for the manufacturer will retain every dealer from one year to the next. This calculates to a 100% rate of customer retention ergo a 100% rate of transactional dependability.

Conversely, the retail mattress industry provides an example of salespeople who face a high rate of customer turnover. The average consumer buys a mattress once every fifteen years or so. Therefore, the odds of a buyer returning to the same location, let alone the same salesperson, are so negligible that it would be best to presume 0% customer retention. The salesperson must, by necessity, accept responsibility to generate *every* transaction, which calculates to a 100% rate of transactional responsibility, essentially zero transactional dependability.

The manufacturer sales representative role in which I worked presented very high transactional dependability; I succeeded because my clients were successfully selling my product even if I wasn't.

Essentially this means that transactional responsibility is being transferred down the supply chain. The transfer of transactional responsibility is not something enjoyed only by manufacturer sales representatives, but a luxury afforded managers and executives for whom salespeople work. It's the reason that so many salespeople aspire to the role of sales manager, to escape the heat.

It's a much easier job and leadership role when the onus of transactional responsibility is on someone else. Of the thousands of sales managers in the world, many have never carried a sales briefcase or worked in a role where compensation is dependent on performance. These last comments are not an indictment of sales managers, but a call for inspiration and, to be clear, thousands of managers are highly competent salespeople and leaders.

The point is that high transactional dependability also creates *transactional dependence*, the *level to which the salesperson or manager is dependent on another salesperson or customer for transactions*. The further the salesperson, manager, or executive is from the sales heat, the more they must rely on others to generate transactions. This should send a warning sign to anyone employing salespeople in a role of high transactional dependability because it infers, if not proves, that *sales results are not the ideal measurement of performance quality*. Again, my experience proved it; I was a lousy salesman getting good results in spite of myself, something an astute manager should have known.

It begs the question whether a salesperson is even necessary in a role of high transactional dependability. If the product dealer is committed, why have boots on the ground? Who needs a salesperson when a phone call, webinar, or internal customer service representative will do? The obvious answer is that a field salesperson is able to deliver a needed personal touch, but hardly enough to justify the cost of employing a professional golfer who can't advance the sales cause.

The real answer lies in the salesperson's ability to impact transactional dependability, which is more than a rate of customer retention. Transactional dependability was defined earlier as the rate of *transactional* customer retention, emphasis on the transactional added here. Thus the rate of transactional dependability is not as simple as measuring the loss (or gain) of direct customers, but must include the volume of purchases *from* those customers.

The car manufacturer might not "lose" any dealers but discovers, through calculations of market averages, that without the proper marketing and sales support, overall sales volume to a large network of dealers declines by an average of 10% annually. Therefore, the rate of transactional dependability is not 100% as based on the retention of dealers, but is reduced to 90% based on the predictability of repeat transactions in the absence of intervention.

The goal and success of the salesperson is now defined by the retention of transactions and growth of them to offset losses due to attrition. Theoretically, if a salesperson is unable to impact transactional dependability, then arguably there is no value in the staffing. The good news is that quality sales performance can positively affect transactional dependability through skilled intervention.

Increasing High Dependability through Intervention

Shift your thought from cars to the manufacturer rep for a brand of cooking knives. Unlike the relationship between the car dealer and manufacturer, there is a diminished degree of loyalty and brand commitment. The same is true for the consumer. Whereas the car buyer enters the dealership with a brand in mind, the decision-making bias of the knife shopper entering the store is unpredictable.

There are two likely decision-making paths for the consumer, one of which includes a brand preference and the other a snap decision made in the heat of the shopping moment. If it is the latter, almost anyone would agree that at least some consumers will seek advice from the store salesperson, thus establishing an opportunity for supply chain sales influence. If this is a little confusing, let's try some mathematics.

Suppose 50% of all consumers enter the store with a preferred brand of cooking knife in mind. Of the remaining 50%, suppose half of them will say they are "just looking" when asked if they need help. This leaves half of the remaining shoppers, which is 25% of the original total that will be influenced by the advice they receive from someone in the store. This means that the manufacturer sales rep should intervene to influence the sales preference not with the consumer, but with the retail knife *seller*, who is seen as the higher authority for 25% of undecided consumers.

The manufacturer sales rep's challenge is therefore to make two levels of sale. The first is the *commitment sale* to the reseller where dialogues occur with executives and managers for purchasing agreements, marketing plans, inventory levels, product training, and more. The second sale is something we will call in economic terms *transactional advocacy*. Transactional advocacy occurs when *a supplier impacts the behaviors of individual resellers to create brand or product advocacy that increases transactional dependability*. Thus, after gaining the proper program commitment to the product, the second sale is with the retail salespeople who have direct access to consumers.

This provides a tidy illustration to create higher transactional dependability through intervention where it had seemed little opportunity existed. Just for fun, let's take our knife selling scenario one step further. Suppose the retail knife reseller's total sales volume for all knife brands combined equals $25,000. If this were the case, the manufacturer sales rep for knives might conclude that the target sales objective is the 25% share that can be had by influencing salespeople at the retail sales level…or $6,250. If the manufacturer representative is only earning $1,000 in purchases per year, intervention could feasibly raise sales by $5,250.

Proper sales intervention impacts sales results indirectly by providing training, coaching, and sales assistance that drives the confidence of retail salespeople. Transactional dependability through customer retention begins with commitment at the managerial decision-making level of the customer, but is enhanced through strategic intervention to create transactional retention and growth by influencing salespeople closer to the "heat" of low transactional dependability.

Elevating Low Transactional Dependability

The scale works both ways. In some sales roles of low transactional dependability, salespeople can raise the value of this economic sales indicator. For example, a salesperson for a car dealer might expect to retain very few customers and even expect zero transactional dependability. This presumption unfortunately leads to botched sales opportunities.

Curtis is the latest and perhaps the most splendid example of sales botchery in my car buying life. He is one of five different salespeople over an eighteen-year period who have leased me cars. Each knew at the moment a contract was signed the exact second a new car would be needed, the most vital piece of information to elevate transactional dependability. This piece of information provides a rare sales opportunity not enjoyed by others in the retail sale of durable goods.

Your refrigerator might last two years or twenty. Your washer might last five years or fifteen (although I think the manufacturers have magically created a level of obsolescence that causes the machines to break down three days after the five-year warranty expires). The sales cycle on most durable home goods is unpredictable. On the other hand, the lease buyer of a car has given the salesperson a piece of invaluable information; specifically the very millisecond the lease expires!

Unlike the luckless mattress salespeople who have found themselves in inescapable roles of zero transactional dependability with little chance for a repeat buyer (although the opportunity might exist for a referral campaign to relatives and friends of their buyers), the car salesperson can do something about it. The lease provides an opportunity for career security based on the cultivation of lasting sales relationships. Automobile salespeople can evolve to affect and elevate transactional dependability. This is a lesson Tonto, a Ford salesman, learned early in his career.

Tonto also happens to be an extraordinary golfer. You can bump into him at the Harbor Shores golf course in Benton Harbor, Michigan, for a chat about golf, sales, and life. In between golf lessons, we discussed his approach to building lasting relationships with customers, some to whom he has sold cars repeatedly for many years. His approach to sales, to be honest, wasn't particularly innovative although deeply empathetic, but his belief in relationships was unique among car salespeople. He retained files on his buyers and knew them by name when they came to his dealership. He discovered the reasons behind the purchase for each car. He told me, "I would sell the whole family." He saw the sale not as a transaction, but instead a lasting relationship. Curtis did not and botched a relationship opportunity.

As a show of appreciation after my car purchase, I sent Curtis a copy of one of my books on selling along with a thank-you note. After driving my new Lexus for one week, I remembered that a verbal commitment I heard (or thought I did) was not fulfilled. It was no big deal, but I called Curtis to ask him about it. I received no return call. I received no thank-you note. There has been no direct follow-up from Curtis for nearly two years and I expect none will be coming. His behaviors matched the behaviors of the four other salespeople from whom I leased cars. No follow-up. No thanks. No nothing. And, most importantly, no next sale. All five had opportunities to reach out and get a repeat sale and all five botched the opportunity. It is a certainty I will buy another Lexus; it is uncertain from whom I will buy it.

Curtis and Tonto offer a remarkable study in contrasting sales performance. Curtis virtually ignored a buyer who will likely purchase an identical brand two or three times in the next ten years; Tonto provided thank-you notes, birthday cards, and an occasional phone call to past customers. Curtis has a job; Tonto built a career. Curtis accepts a role of low transactional dependability; Tonto creates high transactional dependability through client loyalty and as the car salesperson to a family. Tonto is not alone.

Thousands of salespeople elevate transactional dependability in roles traditionally associated with low dependability. They create referral business where word of mouth among customers' families and friends generate new (and easier!) sales opportunities. Remodelers create referral marketing programs and even strive for a backlog of business so they can create negotiation power, which is to say a remodeler who is booked for months in advance has more ability to hold pricing in the face of combative negotiations.

As conditions of sales environments, low and high transactional dependability create very different challenges. High transactional dependability offers methods for the competent salesperson to increase that dependability. Low transactional dependability is not a condition that necessarily leads to victimization as Tonto proved by building loyalty with trusting customers who returned for repeat purchases over many years.

The real power of these lessons on high and low transactional dependability lies within the actions of each salesperson. You can't control the situations, but you can control your responses to them to achieve deeper levels of career security. Tonto provides the example of the salesperson elevating his career security by positively enhancing transactional dependability where little is believed to exist. The manufacturer sales rep also raises career security by affecting transactions closer to the sales heat, like our knife salesman.

These examples demonstrate that a skilled salesperson can elevate the levels of dependability with strategic intervention. If the salesperson, however, ignores the potential impact to be made on transactional dependability, then career security becomes highly contingent on selling circumstances.

Without intervention, a solid argument can be put forth that a salesperson who thrives in a role of low transactional dependability is likely to have more security than a salesperson operating in an environment of high transactional dependability; simply stated the former has proven the ability to generate transactions repeatedly out of necessity while the latter can, well…golf.

Creating Career Security

Transactional dependency is the corollary to transactional dependability. Dependability is the pleasure of receiving easy sales; dependence means the fear of relying on them. It's two ends of the same knife, one a tool and the other a dangerous weapon. This is why I consider myself lucky that I worked for a company on the verge of bankruptcy while being yelled at for product defects. I later saw the "after picture" of transactional dependence that would have occurred had I settled comfortably into my original career path and not benefited from the fortune of later lessons.

The "after picture" revealed itself during an interview with a candidate seeking a position as a manufacturer sales representative. He had been a sales manager for nearly twenty-five years and looked the part, polished and articulate. His pedigree included work with a veritable who's who of leading brands for the construction industry, every one of them a household name. I believe most untrained interviewers would have jumped at the chance to hire him.

Unfortunately for the sales candidate, he had been demoted during the economic depression of the early twenty-first century. He was not fired, but merely moved to a sales role for a roofing dealer where he would be expected to build a customer base of contractors in a major Midwestern city. He could no longer rely on the benefit of transactional dependability granted by his role as a sales manager. Most importantly, his compensation would be directly tied to sales results.

I asked why he was looking for a sales job even though he had already been offered one by his employer. He bluntly responded, "There isn't enough time to build a client base with the commission structure offered." Given the fact that nearly forty other salespeople were achieving lofty success within the confines of the same commission structure with his employer, it's fair to say the candidate was interviewing to capture the guaranteed salary offered by my client, a manufacturer, rather than face the challenge of transactional responsibility. He was not offered the position and called me a few weeks later to request what he called an "exit interview."

After providing the rote, courteous response that "you had been seriously considered; it was a tough decision; it came down to you and one other candidate…" he requested more feedback. He felt the interview had gone poorly and wanted to know what suggestions were available to help him improve his skills in that area. It was a tough moment and I asked how much truth he wanted. He assured me he wanted it all.

He needed to improve his selling skills, not his interviewing skills. His answer that there was "not enough time" indicated a level of fear about his own selling skills or financial stability or both. He wasn't prepared after a twenty-five-year career to accept the challenge of an incentive-based compensation plan.

He didn't need a new job to produce security; he needed real career security. He needed to wean himself from dependence on his sales employees who were creating all the heat and transactions.

If he had been made an offer by my client, the new position would have continued masking deficiencies in his selling skills that had been concealed for years. I suggested that his time prospecting for a new job would be better spent prospecting for new clients in the sales role he had been offered. If he believed he had the credentials to manage salespeople, then he had to believe he had the credentials to sell. If not, then he needed to build his credentials.

High and low transactional dependability roles are a function of selling conditions, not skill levels. *Sales Economics* provides behavioral skills and measurements to control outcomes regardless of the role a salesperson occupies in the profession. It's not the sales circumstances that determine your fate; it's how you respond to them. A salesperson who worries about the consequences of losing their job should be investing more energy to build the skills that endure for a career.

3

Pricing Fallacies:
Starting Points, MSRPs,
and Best Offers

The Price Objection

There is a funny scene in Monty Python's *Life of Brian* when Brian, the savior of mankind, is standing over a waiting crowd eager to hear his words of wisdom. He assures them he has nothing important to say. As he speaks, they not only hang on to his every word, when he says, "You've got to think for yourselves. You are all different." In unison the crowd chants, "Yes! We. Are. All. Different."

I'd like to think that behavioral economists would get a special chuckle out of the satirical moment. Microeconomic theory offers the law of supply and demand that presumes human beings all behave the same way—as in "We. Are. All. Alike." We *are* all different, and yet traditional pricing theory of economics struggled with this presumption, and in fact takes the opposite approach.

The "Law" of Supply and Demand

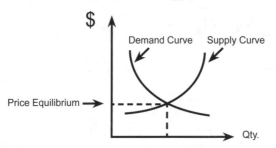

Figure 3.1: The supply curve illustrates the motivation of market producers to allocate more assets toward increased supply as the price rises. The demand curve illustrates the reduction in demand that results from escalating prices. *Price equilibrium* is predicted to be the level at which the two curves intersect to balance pricing and the allocation of production resources.

The theory states that sellers will eagerly produce and sell more of a product as the price rises, less when the price drops. Conversely, buyers will buy more of a product as the price drops, less when the price rises. This creates the supply and demand curves (Figure 3.1). The prevailing theory states the final price at which the market sells is the "equilibrium" point at which the two curves intersect. The theory feels right to salespeople because they encounter the ubiquitous pressure of the "price objection," an indicator in their minds that the market is happening to them.

The price objection is a universal challenge that starts at the beginning of a sales career and endures for the duration, but is not a market condition. Behavioral economics proves that buyers hardly behave with consistency and therefore demonstrates that market equilibrium is a fallacy, as in *people are all different.* I have already asserted that salespeople are also like buyers, humans that hardly behave with consistency. Behavioral sales economics illustrates how sales bias and different sales approaches become highly influential determinants of price levels.

Pricing Theory Was Wrong

I sat in an advanced economics class many years ago and recall that Daniel Fusfeld, former chair of the Economics Department at the University of Michigan, casually told a group of students that the law of supply and demand is obviously not true. The law of supply and demand is an excellent theoretical construct with elements of truth, but fails to illustrate the full, more complicated reality of pricing levels. He asserted that costs determined price. That lecture haunts me today because I made the mistake for years of repeating my mentor's words and now believe his assertion, or my recollection of it, to be half true at best.

Hundreds of my clients over the years have based their pricing models on gross margin markup. My professor claimed correctly that pricing at clothing stores, restaurants, and wholesale distributors is based on markup. The inference of his claim, at least to me, means that pricing will not only be determined by markup, but that laws of financial physics would determine *appropriate* pricing levels that every seller would achieve. In other words, his claim infers that markup would be consistent and pricing levels therefore stable and predictable.

Deeper examination of pricing reveals that markups between different companies are inconsistently applied. Not only are pricing levels inconsistent between companies in spite of nearly identical cost structures, they are different *inside* of them. Two sales reps in the same organization, sometimes working fifteen feet from each other, are selling the same product at very different levels. QED (quod erat demonstrandum, Latin for "it can be demonstrated"), a *consistent* markup to cost is not the final determinant of prices.

Price levels are therefore not determined exclusively by the supply and demand curve intersection, nor by consistent markup above costs. The conclusion left to draw is that prices are arbitrarily and uniquely applied by companies and by individual people within them. At the very least, a consistent formula for pricing theory is elusive. Economists have sought answers to additional questions about pricing theory over the years and address them with anecdotal theories.

For example, *elasticity of demand* is a concept that asserts some products are more price sensitive than others. The price of food is said to be "highly elastic" because shifts in price allow buyers to select alternatives—e.g., hamburger is cheaper than filet mignon but still allows the consumption of red meat. Crude oil is highly inelastic because there are fewer substitutes and therefore shifts in pricing have only small impacts on demand. This theory and others again leave us with the same problem—i.e., the expectation of consistency. In other words, theories imply that individuals will all perform alike. Economic concepts addressed the simplistic flaws in foundational theories, but still presumed that humans behave similarly and predictably. They don't. Humans are unpredictable and have unique idiosyncrasies of behavior that affect, among other things, pricing levels.

This is where the work of brilliant pioneers in the field of behavioral economics have provided enlightenment. Richard Thaler illustrated numerous situations in which unique tastes, situations, and beliefs defy logic and pricing levels. In one example, he talks about a friend who complains about the hay fever he gets when he mows his lawn. The suggestion is that he pay a kid to do the job for $10; he refuses to fork over the money while, at the same time admitting he wouldn't mow someone *else's* lawn at twice the price. If a buyer discovers a $10 discount is available on a product at the same brand of store a few miles away, the drive feels worth it on a product priced at $45, but hardly worth the effort on a $500 product; same discount and travel time, but a different perception of value.

I experienced a similar lapse in logic during a trip to my local Costco where a special discount of fifteen cents per gallon of gas creates high demand at their pumps. Like other members of this retail giant, I pulled up on a Saturday morning and ran into a veritable traffic jam. The line for each pump was five to seven cars deep. Pulling into the pileup would cost me twenty minutes of my life.

I should have asked myself why anyone would invest that much time to save so little money. I should have wondered if the waiting customers would work for an hourly salary of $4.50 per hour, because waiting in line twenty minutes to save

$1.50 on ten gallons of gas is doing just that. In that moment of epiphany, I would have decided to skip the line and go to a no-wait gas station three blocks away. I *would* like to say that was how my mind worked, but it didn't.

In fact, I did pull out of the parking lot to head to another gas station. The decision, however, was not based on cold-blooded analysis, but just the opposite. I am impatient and didn't feel like waiting. After filling my tank, I took satisfaction knowing I would still have been stuck in the Costco line. My decision wasn't rational; it was emotional. I paid a higher price needlessly, albeit happily. These are the types of conundrums that behavioral economics seeks to answer.

Gas has long been considered to be a product of very inelastic demand; that is, the changing price of a gallon does little to change the demand or consumption of this precious commodity. However, as proven by the line at Costco, some people will drive out of their way and wait thirty minutes to save a few pennies per gallon while another is willing to spend 8% more to save a few precious moments of life. Clearly pricing theory is a complicated matter.

The Fallacy of the Market

The real issue here is not to define new models in pricing theory vis-à-vis the buyer, but instead illustrate the pricing bias and fallacies of the seller. As noted, the fundamental theories of many economic principles rely on the false presumption that people behave consistently. Economists are not alone in this presumption. Salespeople, too, believe and act as if buyers are a robotic and logical homogenous group of people who behave with predictable consistency. It is what salespeople call the "market." I learned this during travels to hundreds of North American cities where salespeople consistently say, "My market is different."

I let those words linger after hearing this common lament and then say, "Let me guess. It's ultracompetitive pricewise."

"Yeah!" they respond. "You ain't kidding."

"I suspect buyers aren't very loyal and will drop you to save a few pennies."

"Yes!" they say with rising enthusiasm. Finally, someone gets them.

"Probably can't get them to have a quality dialogue with you until they can verify you're going to be competitive, right?"

"Wow," they say, settling in with someone who finally understands their unique world. "Have you worked here before?"

You may read this dialogue and presume it proves the truth that all markets are, in fact, the same because I could predict their similar responses in various markets. This may actually be true. Each market may be similar, but the power in this lesson is recognizing that the people *within* each market behave differently.

The common "market" lament of victimized salespeople is a response to anecdotal experiences that cloud their judgment of buyer behavior in general. Two or three buyers negotiate combatively and the salesperson concludes that the entire market is a batch of price- sensitive, robotic buyers all behaving alike. They conclude falsely that the market is happening to them, when it is instead their own false beliefs.

They view the market as a forest without examining each individual tree. The markets are comprised, as the behavioral economists have proved, of people who are all very different. In each market, some buyers are combative price shoppers and others are fair negotiators; some buyers are loyal while others are not; some buyers have abundant resources at their disposal while others are on a budget; some make decisions based on investment-grade quality while others do not.

As an example, there are raving fans of Nordstrom, a clothing store hardly known for bargains. Admittedly, I shop at Nordstrom because I view clothing as an investment-grade purchase. I'm not buying clothing based on the price of their shirts or slacks, but on my perception of the *life cost* of the clothing. I believe shirts last many years longer from Nordstrom than those purchased at Men's Wearhouse or Jos. A. Banks. Notice that I use the word "believe." I could be wrong; I might be right. It is my belief that drives me to pay more because, while paying more in the short term, I believe I save money in the long run. Clearly millions of men are not of the same mindset and happily keep the goods flowing at the other clothing stores.

A reader might assert that the perception of quality is only in my head and I wouldn't argue. What I know is that I won't wait in line to save three dollars on a tank of gas, but I will pay over one hundred dollars for a shirt. Someone else will wait in line, but not spend one hundred dollars for a shirt. As we look at the market from thirty thousand feet, it is a homogenous group of buyers. As we move closer to the ground, we discover unique factors affecting buying decisions and willingness to pay higher prices, which is exactly the point.

Nordstrom, the Men's Wearhouse, Jos. A. Bank, other retailers, and online shopping are available in the *same* markets.

The "market" is not a cohesive set of individuals all behaving identically. The markets may be similar, but individual decision-making is not and there is a place for all these sellers in each market. The sooner a salesperson comes to accept this truth, the sooner the salesperson will increase pricing and sales margin, which is really the point of behavioral sales economics.

You can't analyze buying decisions using only a theoretical model. You must introduce the human equation into the dialogue. This means not only analyzing how buyers think and buy, but *how sellers think and sell.*

Milk, Eggs, and Widgets

My business-to-business clients frequently share a riddle: "Why do people constantly negotiate with us, but would never expect to negotiate on the price of milk or eggs at a grocery store?" The answer is easy: *You tell them to!*

An analysis of pricing levels and margins of numerous companies revealed the remarkable consistency of their pricing *inconsistency*. In other words, companies didn't just price differently between each other, but price differently within their own ranks. In numerous studies, salespeople within the same organizations were polled and asked the price at which they would sell five core construction products to professional contractors. The answers, *from salespeople working for the same company*, varied greatly, even between two salespeople sitting at desks within arms' reach of each other. In other words, the competition you face is not only the competing supplier in your market, but the other salesperson in your own organization!

An analysis of price levels at various organizations for one category of products—we'll call them "widgets" (a term commonly believed to have originated by economists, using it as a generic placeholder for any product analysis)—revealed telling data. The prices charged to individual customers vary dramatically from one to another without objective justification for discounts.

Figure 3.2 provides actual pricing levels that were charged by a salesperson working for a distributor of hard goods. The profit margins are indiscriminately applied. Prices for the highest volume client were greater than the prices for many of the lower volume buyers. Most businesspeople would predict that, if pricing is subject to negotiation, buyers who purchase larger volumes will, on average, get better pricing. Buyers who purchase less would pay more. This is not the case in this actual example emblematic of numerous companies studied.

This is a powerful case that illustrates the impact of seller behavior and, more importantly, mindset—i.e., behavioral sales economics. Pricing levels were based on one-on-one dialogues between sellers and buyers that resulted in "opinion pricing," which suggests prices are determined by the fears, beliefs, and poor negotiation skills of sellers, not necessarily buyer expectations or demands. Clearly the "market" allows for higher margins, as attested by the pricing paid by the larger volume buyers.

Margin Report for an Individual Sales Performer

Volume Rank	Sales Volume	Margin %	Margin Dollars
1	$ 187,591	24.27%	$ 45,527
2	161,522	19.20%	31,018
3	131,081	18.22%	23,877
4	76 257	26.46%	20,177
5	71,296	18.40%	13,119
6	47,082	24.98%	11,759
7	40,216	18.76%	7,546
8	30,323	24.99%	7,579
9	22,949	20.14%	4,621
10	20,628	28.60%	5,900
11	18,369	19.53%	3,588
12	11,480	17.64%	2,025
13	11,366	22.83%	2,594
14	10,164	37.83%	3,845
15	7,983	23.55%	1,880
16	5,887	19.82%	1,167
17	2,985	40.33%	1,204
18	2,614	9.90%	259
19	2,609	24.63%	642
20	1,529	8.86%	135
Totals	$ 863,931	21.81%	$ 188,463

Figure 3.2: This is an actual margin portrait of a salesperson working for a construction materials distributor. The pricing model illustrates dramatic pricing inconsistency of gross margins, which may or may not be based on justifiable decisions. More likely, it is a phenomenon that should be analyzed as an opportunity for profit enhancement.

The indiscriminate pricing model leads to a host of questions: Are some buyers better negotiators than others? Are salespeople doing customers favors? Do some customers somehow merit a lower price when buying small quantities while others do not? Clearly pricing is a highly subjective matter and behavioral sales economics leads us to the conclusion that salespeople frequently establish pricing based on opinions and emotions. Even if the price deviations are justifiable, it is clear the law of supply and demand is not holding true.

Suggested Pricing Creates Heroes

The reason for these price deviations was revealed during a conversation with the VP of sales and marketing for a lumber dealer. He told me the company software provides "suggested" levels at which staff members should price goods. In his mind, this meant his salespeople should regularly charge at those suggested levels unless an unusual circumstance required an adjustment. He viewed the suggested pricing as the *expectation*.

Sellers, on the other hand, treated the suggested pricing as an *exception*. They believed their contact with customers gave them superior insights into pricing necessity and therefore offered the prices they believed appropriate. Price was not fixed by a strategic profit analysis, but instead bartered during each transaction by salespeople with bias, limited information, and often a stronger incentive to make a sale at low margin than risk losing it at higher profitability.

Pause to think about the milk and eggs riddle again. The same professional buyers who aggressively negotiate the price of machinery, manufacturing components, commodity metals, or professional service fees willingly pay the price of milk and eggs without hesitation at their local grocery. Same buyer, different expectation—an expectation set by the seller! They don't negotiate the price of milk because the cashier is not empowered. Their expectations shift when buying business assets because the VP of sales allowed the price to be a "suggestion." The result is that pricing makes almost no sense, as you can see in Figure 3.3, when some of the smallest volume buyers are receiving the lowest prices.

The practice of negotiating in the business-to-business environment has become entrenched to the point that not only do buyers expect to negotiate, salespeople believe their role is to help the buyer get the best possible deal. After all, the price from the employer was only a *suggestion* and the salesperson uses this flexibility to become the buyer's advocate by adopting a new mindset—the "hero's complex."

Salespeople, even when compensated for increases in margins, will often lower their price as the means to get a sale. Steven Levitt and Stephen Dubner, two very creative economists who co-wrote *Freakonomics*, proved that realtors, while expressly contracted as *seller* representatives, nevertheless make sales driven by selfish motivations that cost their clients potential profits, even if unintentionally. The reasoning is very simple. A small variation to the large price of a home has a small effect on the commission for the realtor. The realtor is incentivized to make an adjustment to the price even though the seller, the client who is supposed to be protected by the realtor, might sacrifice thousands of dollars. There is no reason to suspect it is a practice limited to real estate transactions. It is likely true for salespeople in other roles.

Margin Analysis for an Individual Sales Performer

Volume Rank	Sales Volume	Margin %	Margin Dollars
20	$ 1,529	8.86%	$ 135
18	2,614	9.90%	259
12	11,480	17.64%	2,025
3	131,081	18.22%	23,877
5	71,296	18.40%	13,119
7	40,216	18.76%	7,546
2	161,522	19.20%	31,018
11	18,369	19.53%	3,588
16	5,887	19.82%	1,167
9	22,949	20.14%	4,621
13	11,366	22.83%	2,594
15	7,983	23.55%	1,880
1	187,591	24.27%	45,527
19	2,609	24.63%	642
6	47,082	24.98%	11,759
8	30,323	24.99%	7,579
4	76,257	26.46%	20,177
10	20,628	28.60%	5,900
14	10,164	37.83%	3,845
17	2,985	40.33%	1,204
Totals	**$ 863,931**	**21.81%**	**$ 188,463**

Figure 3.3: A sorted analysis illustrates that sales volume has no bearing on price levels. The questions to ask are: Why? Should higher volume clients expect to be rewarded with volume discounts? Are the lower discounts merited? If so, why? Did final price decisions come down to sales bias?

Behaviors shift when the seller is empowered to lower prices. Armed with negotiation latitude, salespeople proudly state they will do what can be done to honor a request for a lower price. The vice president who allowed sellers to choose the price of widgets as a matter of opinion tacitly encouraged his salespeople advocate for buyers. No longer are sellers focused on maximizing profits for their client, the employer. Instead they pose as heroes to buyers.

Salespeople given the choice of holding their price and risking the loss of a sale, particularly when a small compensation shift occurs in spite a larger impact on profits, feel safer sacrificing profits to ensure the sale. The salesperson might first offer a starting price, but quickly caves to negotiation pressure to salvage the sale. Predictably, the salesperson defends their decision with a self-professed expert opinion about the situation. The salesperson never considered the "suggested" price as the final price in the first place.

The reason you pay the set price for a dozen eggs or a gallon of milk without negotiation is that nobody told the cashier to sell at a suggested price. It *is* the price. The cashier is not posing as a hero who will save you, the buyer, money; they are instead processing orders at a pre-established price that is calculated to achieve the profit objectives of the grocery store. Many products are not sold with established pricing standards, but instead with overt signals that tell buyers to expect negotiation latitude and lower prices.

The price is no longer a set number; it's a starting point. The manufacturer's suggested retail price (MSRP) is provided with the clear message to buyers they would be foolish to actually buy at that level. A used car sits on the side of the road with a sign that says, "$2,800 OBO," shorthand for "or best offer," telling the potential buyer the seller has no expectation to get the asking price. Salespeople deliver "bids" to buyers with the request to get the "last look before any final decisions are made," a clear indicator that the price is negotiable. In the world of selling, instead of prices we deliver "starting points." Why? More importantly, if salespeople are given flexibility in negotiations, how are they making pricing decisions?

The answer: bias.

The salesperson operates with numerous incentives to lower prices including: fear of losing a sale or customer, financial needs, pressure from supervisors to succeed, pride, and the hero's complex, to name a few. Negotiation empowerment and latitude virtually ensure unnecessary loss of profits. Starting points and "suggested" prices produce an army of salespeople who negotiate with their own employers for a discount on behalf of the buyer. "Besides," the salesperson secretly tells himself, "my customers are now loyal buyers exclusive to me, the hero who gives them price breaks."

QED, based on the data and rationale discovered in dialogues, proves that *sales behavior and bias determines lots of prices, not necessarily demand, elasticity, or margins.* More importantly, it proves that a lot of pricing decisions are made at the last second before the transaction is complete, proving that pricing is a subject for behavioral sales economics where the bias of a salesperson is the real determinant of price.

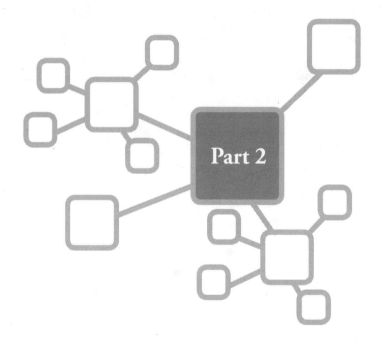

Part 2

BEHAVIORAL
SALES ECONOMICS

4

Beat the Price Objection

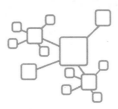

The Power of a Point

The buyer negotiates at the last minute with the casual request for "a little help on the price with a percentage point." The pressure of the request, no matter how casual and regardless of sales experience, causes heart palpitations and anxiety. The seller announces that he does, in fact, have the authority to sacrifice one point. He offers it to the buyer and proudly earns the sale.

Pop quiz!

What are the implications of the sales decision?

A. A precedent has been set and your future prices won't be taken at face value.

B. The seller loses between 10% and 33% of the profit.

C. The buyer is left wondering if he could have gotten more.
D. Lower personal service levels will be later justified.
E. All of the above.

It's a funny thing about a single percentage point on the price of a sale. That little discount creates a lot of disadvantages for the seller. A sales precedent has been set and credibility is damaged. Future offers will no longer be treated as prices like a gallon of milk or the dozen eggs at a grocery store, but instead as starting points. The price is *proven* to be negotiable.

Many salespeople recognize their employer sells at targeted gross margins, but neglect to recognize the larger financial picture. A salesperson working for a $100 million company (based on the P & L percentages as shown in Figure 4.1) should understand that the same company, operating at a 25% gross margin, actually has $25 million, not $100 million, of operating expenses to allocate. The $25 million gets eaten up quickly with overhead, capital, labor, and miscellaneous expenses. The small percentage remaining is the profit… before tax. The sales motivation must be profit before volume; nobody needs practice working for free (or at a loss!). The goal is profitability.

Profit/Loss Statement for Acme Sales

Revenue (100%)		$1.00
Material (COGs)	.75	
People	.11	
Capital Expenses & Overhead	.08	
Miscellaneous	.03	
Total Cost of Operations (97%)		.97
Gross Profit (3%)		.03

Figure 4.1 – Simple P & L Statement for Acme Sales
In this simplified P&L statement for Acme Sales Organization, the company gross profit, after the cost of goods, people, capital investments, and other expenses, is 3%. A salesperson who sacrifices a single percentage point on the sale is not giving up 1% of the sale, but actually 33% of the company profit...before tax. One objective of sales economics is to demonstrate skills that maximize profits.

Less obvious to most salespeople are the dramatic financial implications of a one point discount. After the cost of goods and expenses, depending on the industry and the quality of the company leadership, the gross profits of a company will usually range from 3% to 10%. Therefore the small percentage point that the salesperson gives up is not a "single point," but between ten percent (for companies grossing 10% profit) to one-third of company profit (for companies grossing 3%).

After the salesperson offers the 1% concession, the remaining challenge is one for behavioral economics. The sales hero feels confident they have provided a valued service to the buyer. On the other hand, the buyer naturally wonders what would have happened had he not asked for a better deal and left money on the table. He also presumes the price was artificially inflated in the first place; if there was room to move, after all, why not just give the best price up front?

The most surprising implication of the 1% discount is the nagging feeling left for buyers that they didn't win—that perhaps they could have gotten another point or two. That's right! The only way your buyers know they received your best price is when you look them straight in the eye and promise you have no room to negotiate. Ideally, the best solution is to prevent the price negotiation in the first place.

There is another surprising outcome of the discounted price. In numerous surveys with salespeople, they are asked, "If you lower your price, does it diminish the level of service you feel you need to bring to the customer?" A surprising number of salespeople agree that a combative negotiator wins on price, but loses because the salesperson feels a discounted price justifies discounted services. The risk of diminished service levels is a lost client or a dissatisfied one who writes public one-star and two-star online reviews. A lower price should never be delivered with the expectation that lower service levels are justifiable. Yet right or wrong, it happens.

Given all of the negative implications of a small discount, it would appear that the best thing a salesperson can do, or at least strive to, is hold the price at a fair level for the supplier to protect profitability, justify high quality service levels, and *as the means to inspire price confidence for the buyer.*

The answer to the pop quiz is: E. All of the above.

The bigger, unexamined problem is the original impetus for the price reduction or, as we say in sales parlance, the "price objection."

Dirty Water

The price objection is like dirty water at the mouth of the river. Imagine a team of engineers and workers trying to eliminate the pollution of the Mississippi River at the delta in New Orleans. Silly and impossible. The pollution at the mouth of the river is created upstream from factories, oil discharge, litter, and other pollutants. No matter how much energy you put into cleanup at the end, you won't fix the system. Likewise, if you want to beat the price objection, you need start earlier—upstream—in the sales process.

The pop quiz in the previous section left out a lot, notably everything that happened *before* the request for a discount. It's too late to clean up the pollution at the mouth of the river and too late to fix perceptions of price at the last minute. The price must be justified with sales behaviors early in the sales process.

The price objection is created by sales behaviors at the start when buyers, anxious to minimize sales interaction and gain as many prices as possible, demand bids from numerous suppliers. Sellers, fearing the loss of an opportunity, take the bait and willingly reduce themselves to commodity status by delivering complete, accurate pricing with incomplete, inaccurate information. Proper discovery might have revealed opportunities for higher margins, or the sale of additional products and services. A quality presentation and engagement with other associates within the seller's organization might have inspired more confidence in the buyer to justify a higher price. Before any of this occurs, problems in the ecosystem of pricing were created when price levels were mere "suggestions" to the seller. Salespeople might deny their performance created the predictable price objection but, by the time the price is delivered, it's too late. Speed kills sales.

The seller should have acquired more information to determine appropriate product needs and service levels. The seller should have assessed the buyer's larger intentions and challenges. The seller likely failed to protect himself from combative negotiations by neglecting to prospect and create alternative opportunities—i.e., it's difficult to walk away from a negotiation when you have few other options in your pipeline. In short, the price objection might be a function of the market, but is more likely a function of behavioral sales economics. The buyer didn't cause the price objection; the seller's performance virtually assured it.

Obviously negotiation skills are important and provide tactics to cope with the price objection after it arises although, as Levitt and Dubner proved in *Freakonomics*, skilled sales negotiators still sometimes believe it's better to lose a price negotiation and win a sale. The point is that the price objection can be mitigated and even eliminated when the entire ecosystem of pricing is properly managed upstream with better internal policies, improved sales processes, and effective negotiation skills.

I learned anyone, even me as a supposed expert on sales, can make this mistake as I incompetently demonstrated when a vice president phoned me to discover my fee structure. He said that two of his sales managers had seen my work and were enamored with my capabilities. He simply wanted to create a budget and, believing he was very interested, I took the sales process for granted. I forgot that the vice president himself had never seen my work. I presumed that he knew as I did—that I was the perfect man for the job—except that he didn't. I forgot to do my job and gave him a price…on the phone…without asking a single discovery question.

I did not get the sale.

I didn't follow the selling process I teach every day and lost the opportunity because there was no justification for the asking price. Instead of understanding his situation and hearing the outcomes he had in mind, I presumed we both knew what outcomes would occur. I presumed he had the same objectives as my other clients. Instead of understanding his challenges, I went right to my preconceived notion of a solution. Speed killed my sale and I was the one pressing the accelerator.

Behavioral economics outlines the factors that influence decisions from the *buyer's perspective*. In this case, however, the process needs to be examined from the *seller's perspective*. My performance was the determinant of the sales outcome, not the buyer's bias. Behavioral sales economics requires you to analyze how decisions are influenced, not just by customer bias, but by your behaviors as the seller. If you want to beat the price objection, you need to start upstream, a process that begins long before the price is delivered.

The Law of Pricing

You will never know the joy, power, and satisfaction of holding your price and winning a sale until you have held your price and lost one. The previous sentence is not an opinion; it's a law.

If your first instinct is to consider lowering your price when confronted with a request for a discount, then you will never discover whether you can hold the price. If you are never willing to walk away from a sale because you are always willing to negotiate, then you will never discover whether you can get your best price. The only way to get your asking price is to, at some point in your career, hold firm. It's a law.

There are salespeople who go through entire careers without discovering this powerful truth. Astoundingly, they meet the price objection decades into the profession and their response is still the rote, ineffective hero's lament, "Let me see what I can do." The next step for the salesperson is to pass the buck up the chain of command to a supervisor or vendor. In this way the salesperson becomes a hero to the buyer and falsely believes she has saved her reputation while inadvertently damaging it because although a sale might be made, as noted earlier, credibility is destroyed.

The largest problem is that buyers who are given a discount are left wondering. As noted earlier and a fact worth repeating: the only way buyers can know if they received your best price is when you tell them. It's a fact of behavioral economics for both seller and buyer. Therefore, it's a law: the only way you will ever know if you can get your asking price is by holding it.

Incompetent Negotiators

It's no secret that professional buyers attend seminars, practice clever negotiation techniques, and strive to keep salespeople off guard. It's the buyer's job. This places salespeople who aren't well-trained negotiators at a disadvantage, particularly when forced to negotiate with incomplete information. If nothing else, the salesperson has no idea what emotions the buyer is feeling. More often than not, the seller hasn't conducted adequate discovery. The biggest problem is that buyers use the seller's fear of the competition to win.

The buyer, unlike the salesperson, has full view of the market and pricing. The seller is not privy to the offers competitors have made and, even if the seller has provided information on competitors' offers, the information is sometimes a strategic negotiation tactic by the buyer. I observed this firsthand when watching the buyer for my client cleverly manipulate a seller with pricing information.

The potential buyer for $20 million worth of roofing products told an anxious sales representative on the phone, "You are within a dollar per square." (The "square" is a 10' x 10' unit by which roofing is sold.) Without hesitation, the manufacturer's salesperson sprang into action and assured the buyer he would see what he could do. The phone rang thirty minutes later and the seller offered to reduce the price an additional fifty cents, but not the full dollar requested.

Did you catch the little trick there? I noted that the salesperson couldn't get the full dollar *requested*. Was it requested? Might the buyer have paid the originally quoted price? There was never really a request, but instead a casual statement delivered to a fearful salesperson.

What the manufacturer's rep did not discover was that he had already been forty cents *lower* per square and was now priced ninety cents below any competitor. It was a clever ploy by the buyer, who was not really lying. The seller was, in fact, within a dollar. The buyer didn't mention that the seller was already cheaper, but knew the statement would leverage sales fear. Fifty cents might not seem like a lot because it is less than a point on a product originally priced at $60 per square, 0.833% to be exact. The cost to the supplier, however, was an astounding $166,666 unnecessarily lost in a two-minute phone call!

It's easy to point to this situation and assert that the salesman did a good job because a $20 million sale is too much to risk. However, there is more to the story that the salesman should have considered. The reality is that the buyer was a purchasing agent for a reseller of the manufacturer's product. The sales representative for the manufacturer should have realized that the demand for his popular brand in the market was well established and that the reseller actually *needed* to stock the brand as a means to provide a complete offering to the market.

This roofing sale presented a textbook opportunity to hold firm on price. The seller instead felt the desperation of a much needed sale rather than recognizing his significant negotiation power, a clear case of behavioral sales economics at work in the seller's mind. This was an obvious situation the salesperson should have assessed. The salesperson could have easily assured the buyer there was no room to move and earned the sale, learned a lesson, and preserved significant profit dollars.

What If There Were No Negotiations?

Consider again the vice president's policy for "suggested" pricing levels. What if the price was not a suggestion and salespeople were not permitted to negotiate? Had the roofing salesperson simply stated he was not permitted to lower the price, he would have earned his employer a lot of money. If salespeople were not allowed to negotiate, dramatic shifts in sales performance would occur.

If salespeople were not allowed to negotiate…*prospecting skills would improve.* The underlying reason for a lower price is usually the fear of losing a sale. The only way to mitigate this fear is by creating abundant alternatives in the prospecting pipeline. It is the way a salesperson can achieve the confidence to walk away, specifically by knowing another opportunity awaits with a less combative negotiator.

If salespeople were not allowed to negotiate...*pricing would stabilize and provide a competitive market advantage.* It seems counterintuitive, but a stable pricing structure gives your clients confidence and, more importantly, reduces the risk of market reconnaissance that jeopardizes your brand. Sam, a former owner of a $400 million vinyl window factory, learned serendipitously that his company had been charged a higher price for vinyl compounds than a much smaller company, creating two outcomes.

First, the supplier lost the business and never earned it back. Second, Sam established a strident pricing policy that ensured *his* best customers—measured by volume, loyalty, payment terms, and cost of doing business—would get the best pricing. In other words, pricing was not a negotiated dialogue between a professional purchasing negotiator and an anxious salesperson; pricing was a policy designed to give the company a brand reputation and competitive edge.

If salespeople were not allowed to negotiate...*customers would be confident and satisfied.* A customer who believes they have negotiated the best possible price is a satisfied customer. As noted earlier, the only way a customer really knows your best price was offered is when you say so. We buy the gallon of milk at the price because the checkout clerk is not expected nor permitted to negotiate. Salespeople will get the asking price for your goods if they are not expected nor permitted to negotiate.

Margin Improvement for an Individual Sales Performer

Volume Rank	Sales Volume	Margin %	Margin Dollars
1	$ 187,591	24.00%	$ 45,022
2	161,522	24.00%	38,765
3	131,081	24.00%	31,459
4	76,257	27.00%	20,589
5	71,296	27.00%	19,250
6	47,082	27.00%	12,712
7	40,216	27.00%	10,858
8	30,323	27.00%	8,187
9	22,949	27.00%	6,196
10	20,628	27.00%	5,570
11	18,369	27.00%	4,960
12	11,480	27.00%	3,099
13	11,366	27.00%	3,069
14	10,164	27.00%	2,744
15	7,983	30.00%	2,395
16	5,887	30.00%	1,766
17	2,985	30.00%	896
18	2,614	30.00%	784
19	2,609	30.00%	783
20	1,529	30.00%	459
Totals	$ 863,931	25.41%	$ 219,564

Figure 4.2: If margins were established based on a tiered pricing structure, the slight adjustments would produce large impact. In this scenario, using the same customer base from the previous chapter (Figure 3.2), a tiered pricing structure would yield an increase of $31,101 over the previously earned $188,463, thus producing 3.6% additional profit!

If salespeople were not allowed to negotiate...*profits would rise*. The sales pricing levels depicted in the previous chapter (Figure 3.2) were taken from a larger pool of a pricing model. Figure 4.2 provides a view of a new pricing structure in which companies purchasing in excess of $100,000 receive a discount price calculated at 24% gross margin, which already has been proven to be an acceptable margin, the one being paid by the largest volume customer.

The next tier of customers would receive pricing calculated at 27% gross margin; the last tier at 30%. In honor of my college professor, Daniel Fusfeld, who asserted that margins determine price, here is the half-truth of his theory. This model does not prove the professor right, of course, because margins can be raised slightly to determine if a higher level of pricing will be accepted. Margins might *calculate* the price, but testing the waters of buyer willingness is the real *determinant* of final pricing.

It's also vital to accept that volume alone is not the criterion for pricing decisions. Price levels can take into consideration the cost of doing business, the quality of payment terms, and other factors. The pricing matrices are offered as analytical tools for evaluation. Typically my clients discover that the visual tells a story so compelling that problems and solutions jump off the page. In this case, the matrix is an illustration of a single performer at the company.

A complete analysis (see Figure 4.3) of that company's pricing tiers demonstrated the vast impact of arbitrary pricing policies. Notice the *current* margins at which the company is selling. Surprisingly, the lowest volume customers are purchasing at the most competitive price levels—21.9%.

Clearly it has been proven, by the examples of other clients paying higher prices, money is likely being left on the table.

Margin Enhancement for the Organization

		Current		Projected		
Volume	Total Sales	Avg. GM	GM $$	Tiered QM	GM $$	Difference
Customers Over $20,000	$22,068,401	22.6%	$4,994,988	24.0%	$5,296,418	$301,430
Customers $10,001– $20,000	4,214,200	22.1%	933,099	27.0%	1,137,834	204,735
Customers Under $10,000	3,730,530	21.9%	817,239	30.0%	1,119,159	301,920
TOTALS	$30,013,140	22.5%	$6,745,327	25.2%	$7,553,411	$808,085

Figure 4.3: Behavioral sales economics has proven that sales mindset causes the shift in pricing as much as buyer demands. It has also been demonstrated for this company, as analyzed in the past two chapters, that a high volume customer will pay in excess of 24% gross margin. Therefore testing a new pricing structure at reasonably tiered margins can produce significantly higher profits. In this example, the profit growth equals $808,085 (2.7%) without creating a single new sale!

The consultation for this client, whose pricing structure is similar to numerous others that were examined, was a simple plan to establish a tiered pricing structure based on merit (Figure 4.3). If the top volume customers are willingly paying a near a 25% gross margin, it is reasonable to expect others to follow suit and conservatively seek a projected margin at 24%. A new, sensibly tiered pricing structure most likely builds trust with customers who realize they are being given the best possible pricing up front. More importantly, the company could increase projected profits nearly 3% with the stroke of a pen!

Naturally, there are situations in which a salesperson should negotiate and be equipped with the skills to do so successfully. The question raised here is truly a theoretical construct designed, as economists are prone to do, as a means of considering implications, outcomes, and raising new questions. So, what if salespeople, like a grocery store clerk, were not allowed to negotiate?

If not allowed to negotiate...*salespeople would become more confident in their pricing, achieve a more professional mindset, and develop vital selling skills to justify fair pricing margins while significantly raising profits.* They would have situations, albeit not all, when they get the sale at the original asking price. They would discover ways to slow the process, deliver better presentations, design better proposals, and manage conflict professionally. In short, they would become truly professional salespeople.

As a matter of behavioral sales economics, prior to delivering the price, it is a good preventative practice to let a buyer know that the promise is to offer the best possible deal up front. Later, when buyers negotiate, the salesperson will be in a position to remind them the best price was promised up front...and delivered. Period.

If the first instinct to the price objection is always to barter, then salespeople stand no chance of getting the original asking price leading to a law of price negotiations: *you will never know the joy, power, and satisfaction of holding your price and winning a sale until you've held your price and lost one...*which is easier to do when the price objection is managed upstream.

Price Objection Prevention: Bid Avoidance

Pop quiz!

The phone rings and a potential buyer, someone with whom you have never done business, asks for a price on your services. *(The criterion that the buyer is someone with whom you have never done business is critical to this exercise. If the request for a price is from a client with whom you conduct business regularly, there is usually no need to hesitate because the nature of the relationship, protocols, and expectations have been well established. This is a request from a new prospect who does not currently buy from you.)* Your natural instinct is to learn more. You therefore request a meeting to understand the buyer's situation. The combative buyer tells you that they don't have time, but merely needs to know if you're competitive or not prior to a detailed conversation. If you are "in the ballpark," they assure you there will be a larger dialogue later. What do you do?

A.   Take a pass.

B.   Give them a price because you have nothing to lose.

C.   Define why a meeting is in their best interest.

This situation appears repetitively in the selling world. It's the dirty water upstream. It would be easy, but defensive, to blame buyers. Buyers are trained to speed up the process and minimize time invested with salespeople. It is up to the salesperson to consider new behaviors that address this common situation.

In this case, the price objection will certainly come later if the wrong course of action is taken upstream. If the salesperson quickly provides a price without establishing value, the chance for success is low. The salesperson who answers: B. Give them a price because you have nothing to lose, is later vulnerable to combative price negotiations.

The vice president who called didn't force me to give up my pricing. Like many salespeople, I got excited by an inbound referral and let the endorphins of joy take over instead of consciously slowing down the process. I could have attempted to learn more, but failed. It wasn't the buyer's responsibility to create value; that was my job. No value was established and, just like the dirty water at the mouth of the river, the price objection that came later was created upstream when an unqualified price was offered.

The answer to the pop quiz is: C. Define why a meeting is in their best interest.

My sales management hero, Abe Isaacson, encountered this challenging situation when his pupil, Noah Smith, asked for advice. "The last time I asked you about pricing customers who refused to meet, you suggested that I consider passing on the opportunity. So I got one of those calls from a prospect. I told him I needed more information to bid and that we should meet. The guy got really aggressive and refused to meet. I didn't want to lose the opportunity, so I decided to price it anyway, in spite of your advice."

"What happened?" Abe asked.

"He said my price was too high."

"Did you meet him to deliver your price?" Abe asked.

Sheepishly, Noah admitted that he had not despite the advice from the wise mentor. "I know you told me I should at least require him to meet me after I put the price together if he wouldn't meet me before," Noah said. "He wouldn't."

"And you figured that you might as well give him the price since, after all, you put in the work to create it, right?" Abe asked.

"Yeah," Noah admitted. "I guess I did."

Abe sensed Noah's embarrassment and assured him he did nothing wrong. Noah wasn't buying it. "I did though. You told me to do something that would work and I didn't do it. I should have done it differently."

Abe sat with Noah and placed a hand on his pupil's forearm. "Do you think you're the first person to experience this situation? It's going to happen a lot. I'm proud for you that you're trying to take a different angle this time. Let's rehearse it again, okay?"

"Okay," Noah said with renewed optimism. Abe didn't realize it at the time, but he was contributing to the field of behavioral sales economics. He was taking a common situation and planning a tactical response with the overt plan to observe the outcome. He was simply trying to learn and, as importantly, ensure that his young pupil did the same. As Abe was prone to do, he took out a piece of paper and wrote some notes.

"I call this the 'bid avoidance' presentation," Abe said. "We spoke about it, but here it is in writing. Let's be clear about the situation. We're talking about a new prospect, not an existing customer that gives you the order as a matter of habit, okay?"

"Got it," said Noah while studying the paper (Figure 4.4). "Not that it matters, but what is the difference between a strategy and a tactic?"

The Bid Avoidance Presentation

Situation: A buyer with whom you have not done business requests a blind bid

Strategy: Slow the Process Down

Tactic: The Bid Avoidance Presentation

Key Points to Illustrate:
- Delivery Expectations – e.g., Timing, Frequency
- Service Expectations – e.g., Ordering Protocols, Receiving, After-Sale
- Volume – e.g., One-time versus Ongoing, Duration of Relationship
- Cross-Selling – e.g., Added Products and Services to the Sale
- Goals – e.g., Profit Outcomes, Design Goals, Future Use

Figure 4.4

Abe smiled and said, "There is a big difference. The strategy is a game plan. The plan is to slow the process down. A tactic is a single behavior. There are other ways you can slow the process down. You can conduct a thorough discovery session early in the sales process. You can ask the buyer to commit to a credit dialogue prior to providing a price. In this case, you're asking the buyer to commit to a dialogue before you price. It's the means to be as competitive as possible. It's something you're doing *for the buyer*.

"Tell him that you don't want to waste his time or yours and that you'll be too high without getting more information from him," Abe said.

"Really?" Noah asked with surprise.

"Why not? It's true. If you have no idea how much volume is being purchased, you can't price properly. If you don't know the delivery and service expectations, you can't calculate the costs of doing business properly. If you can't get more information, you have no choice but to err on the side of safety. Tell him you need to meet and use those reasons."

Noah nodded.

"But be prepared for pushback. He's going to ask you why you need to know all that. Your answer is to promise him that you'll be as competitive as possible with the right information. Notice," Abe concluded, "that the outline is intentionally constructed as a means to find *your* voice. The power is not in the script, but instead the content and intention."

Noah nodded again and heard Abe recite the script without looking. "I always say," began Abe, "that I can't be competitive until I know your delivery and service expectations. It matters if this is a one-time sale or a new relationship we'd be launching. We also have other products to add to the mix that might help me become more competitive. No, my friend. I can't do you the disservice. We need to meet for five minutes so I can do the best possible job for you. When is good to meet?"

Noah chuckled at Abe's casual tone. "That works?" he asked.

"Every time," Abe boasted.

"No way," Noah said. "You get the meeting every time?"

"I didn't say that. I said it works every time. It works because I get the information I need. If I get the meeting, I know I have a decent lead on my hands. If not, I presume the buyer is just using me to keep another salesman honest and I might take a pass. Either way, the tactic gives me an outcome I can work with."

"So that counts as working?" Noah asked.

"Do you want to go through the same hassle with another buyer that you experienced with the last one?"

"No," Noah admitted.

"It works for me because it lets me confidently choose my next action. I test a tactic and observe the result. The result tells me what action to take next or what tactic to try differently next time."

The real power of Abe's approach is not in the outcome— i.e., whether or not the buyer agrees to meet—but the attempt. The response you receive from the bid avoidance presentation is a telling moment. Consider the implications of a response from the buyer who hears you explain your reasoning for a deeper dialogue and still rejects the offer. It's a strong indicator that the buyer is not a good lead and that better opportunities exist elsewhere in the market. You still have the option of bidding, but do you really want to invest the time with someone who hasn't offered you the courtesy of an introductory dialogue?

If the price objection is like dirty water at the mouth of the river, the opening dialogue is the source. A lot of frustration and aggravation can be prevented later when the salesperson changes behaviors early in the process. Bid avoidance is a critical selling skill as well as a foundational lesson in behavioral sales economics. Or you can make things even simpler. The next time a buyer says, "I don't have time to meet. Give me a price and show me you're competitive," you are entitled to respond, "Make me an offer and I'll tell you if I can honor it." It is a plausible move in the game of selling. There are many more for you to learn.

5

Negotiate to Win-Win

Back from La-La Land

In *Thinking Fast and Slow*, Daniel Kahneman outlined the work he started with his late, great collaborator, Amos Tversky. Kahneman asserts there are two types of decision-making processes, System 1 and System 2. The former is emotional and intuitive while the latter is logical and unhurried. System 1 is fast; System 2 is slow.

He is fascinated by the idea that decisions are the not the result of cautious, thought-out arguments made by those fictitious cold-blooded buyers, but instead snap judgments based on emotions and bias. For this reason, Kahneman calls System 1 thinking "the real hero" of the book. It is the driver that provides a fun analysis that allows Kahneman to reveal numerous situations in which decisions were made in contradiction to all versions of logic as in a professional investor buying a million shares of Ford because of a nice experience at the auto show.

Malcolm Gladwell later wrote in *Blink* (2005) about situations in which decisions are made on erroneous snap judgments based on hope, fear, dreams, and other bias— i.e., that which Kahneman calls System 1. He also outlines situations in which years of expertise and practice define logical and rational decision-making—i.e., System 2. The first salvo in *Blink* is the story of the Getty Museum in California purchasing a $10 million *kouros* (Greek for "young man") statue after curators examined documents and the work itself. A small sample of the statue was chipped out to chemically verify its dating. Further study validated the provenance and, along with the other vetting techniques, authenticated the legitimacy to establish the collectible as a remarkable version of a popular sculptural design from Greece dated to the sixth century BC.

In the story, various art experts see the statue at its unveiling and instantly declare it a forgery! Naturally the museum curators are concerned and embarrassed, but forced to conduct more research. The telling moment later occurred when a letter supposedly validating the statue's provenance was shown to be a forgery. A postage stamp stuck to a letter of ownership transfer had a meter imprint that was not used when the original letter would have been sent. Later findings validated that the statue's material had been fraudulently prepared to pass a standardized aging test for stone.

On the surface, this story would presumably violate Kahneman's theory of System 1 thinking. After all, the museum did not make a snap decision and worked slowly to validate the authenticity of the purchase. Deeper observation of this story reveals two valuable lessons. The first is that the curators were so emotionally invested with the hope of snagging a rare, priceless work to display that they thought and acted *reactively* while ignoring facts obvious to other experts. They didn't conduct the right diligence and, in fact, exercised System 1's emotionally biased thinking. They saw what they wanted to see, not what was actually there.

The second lesson is that three experts were able to catch the fraud in the blink of an eye, ergo the title of Gladwell's book. It would seem that these experts engaged in System 1 thinking because they were fast in their judgments, but the opposite was true. The experts, although quick to spot the fraud, were slow in their *training*. Their responses were System 2 logic on display in the heat of the moment. It took decades of study in art history to develop the skills that quickly pointed out the fraud. Expertise takes years to accumulate.

Here is the point!

Salespeople endure full careers during which they feel victimized by combative price negotiations. They react to nearly all of them with the same behaviors as the sales hero who advocates for the client. Real sales expertise means developing the System 2 decision-making skills to recognize when a price objection is counterfeit and when it is real. This means slow training and observation to know the difference in the heat of the moment.

System 2 thinking, rational and slow, is not something that occurs only in decision-making moments, but by accumulation of expertise over many years. It's better to possess expertise than be a self-proclaimed expert. Just like art expertise takes years to accumulate, a salesperson needs years of experience to

learn when it is right to negotiate in the heat of the moment…
and how to do it.

Thus, in spite of the "law" that advocates you can only get
your asking price when you hold firm, it would be naïve to
presume that a salesperson should *never* negotiate. Experienced
business leaders know that negotiations do occur and anyone
claiming differently is in la-la land. The "law" still stands that
you will never get your price until you hold it. The real world,
however, presents situations that call for concessions.

Preparing for Battle

The price objection is not a surprise. It's expected because,
as noted earlier, pricing has been "suggested" within an
organization. It's not just a company, but an industry and
profession at large that caves to pressure, falsely perceiving the
price reduction is the competitive edge that earns the sale. This
is a problem economists refer to as the *fallacy of composition*.

Attributed primarily to the late supply-side economist
John Maynard Keynes, the fallacy of composition occurs
when an individual presumes that the thing true for one
individual is therefore true for the whole. The popular example
is the fan who stands at a concert to enjoy a better view and,
paradoxically, presumes this competitive advantage will be
true for everyone. If everyone stands, naturally the view will
be the same as if all were seated, except that everyone will now
be standing. This is how willy-nilly price concessions work.
The epidemic trend was epitomized during a lunch break at a
conference I attended.

"You're the keynote speaker!" one of the diners said with
great surprise and enthusiasm as I joined them at their table.

Another decided to pick my brain by saying, "You were talking about sales, but didn't give me enough about how to deal with *my* market. I get what you're saying, but my problem is my competition. They don't get it. My market has a bunch of lowballers."

A second person agreed! A third said, "We have the same problem." Soon all eight people from different companies were in agreement. They were victims of the "market." This is what economists call the *fallacy of collective terms*. Instead of recognizing individual performance differences and unique seller habits, the presumption is that the entire *market of individual salespeople*—i.e., "lowballers"—behaved as one cohesive unit.

I smiled and listened patiently to their laments before finally offering mock indignation when asking, "Okay! Fess up! Which one of you is the lowballer? Surely someone is lying." Everyone got a good chuckle realizing the irony of their complaints; they were essentially all accusing each other and yet none of them thought they were the problem. This is a prime example of behavioral sales economics where sales bias is created by a presumption is made without established evidence. It was System 1 decision-making at its finest.

The meeting attendees at the table discussed their challenges together. Many stated they were lowering their prices to earn sales and admittedly regretted the lost profits. Others asserted they were losing sales even when prices were lowered to competitors who simply matched pricing. Almost all agreed that they couldn't necessarily verify that better prices actually had been offered by their competitors and, even if they had, whether comparable services were being priced.

So they lowered their prices to gain a competitive advantage and sometimes succeeded, but other times lost to a competitor that might have matched the price. This is the fallacy of composition. A competitive advantage might occur, but is short-lived when the rest of the market follows. One fan stands; they all stand to destroy competitive advantage. One salesperson lowers the price; others follow and competitive pricing advantage is gone.

The Scorpion and the Frog

There is an old fable of unknown origin during which a scorpion enlists the help of a frog to ride across a flowing river on the frog's back. The frog is naturally reticent because he fears for his life, but is reassured when the scorpion promises not to sting him by reminding the frog that would cause them both to perish. It made enough sense for the frog to agree, only to feel a moment into the journey the sting on his back. As his legs go numb and he faces his fate, he looks over his shoulder and incredulously asks the scorpion why he did such a foolish thing that will cause them both to die. The scorpion responds, "It's my nature and what I do. I'm a scorpion."

Buyers test the waters; it's what they do. Reflexively they ask for lower prices, often citing rational reasons that cause sellers to cooperate. Some buyers ask for lower prices with absurd reasoning, leading sellers to harshly assert, "All buyers are liars," which is probably unfair, although it's certainly not a stretch to presume buyers can be misinformed. It's possible the buyer is just challenging the seller as a casual negotiation strategy to ensure the lowest price was being offered—i.e., testing the waters. In other words, claims made by buyers should be treated with a healthy level of curiosity, if not skepticism.

Surely there are times when a lower price should be offered. That being said, *if* salespeople are going to negotiate, they should be equipped with the skills of the trade. System 1 sales thinking—i.e., fast, emotional, and impulsive—creates the hero's mentality and quick responses to "see what can be done" in the face of price objections. System 2 sales thinking—i.e., prepared, factual, and justifiable—requires, like the art history expert, advanced study to prepare for the right sales performance in heat of the moment.

Get to Give Negotiations

The price objection begins simply enough. A buyer casually mentions, whether true or not, that a better deal can be had elsewhere; this puts fear into a salesperson who, even in the absence of evidence, offers concessions. Sometimes all it takes is for the buyer to ask, "Is this really the best you can do?"

This is the moment when logical thinking in the form of preplanned responses is critical. One option, as noted, is to hold your price and see if you can get it. That being said, every salesperson knows the fear of losing a sale and the price reduction they are prepared to offer. Few are equipped with the ability to calmly negotiate rational concessions, an essential skill for sales negotiators.

Consider the position from the buyer's perspective. A buyer who is granted a price reduction without offering any concessions is likely to feel that the original price was a form of gouging. As noted in the previous chapter, future prices are treated as starting points because the previous concession destroyed credibility for the salesperson. Therefore, a price reduction from the seller should always be offered with an attempt at earning a concession in return, if for no other reason than allowing both parties to save face and build a fair compromise.

This is the situation Noah faced when seeking his mentor's advice by asking, "So you once said that you should never lower your price?"

Abe said that wasn't completely true. "The thing I said is that you will never know if you can get your price until you stand firm. There are times when it might be justifiable to lower a price. If that happens, though, you have to make it fair for the buyer," Abe concluded.

"Did you mean fair for the *seller*? Isn't a lower price, by definition, fair for the buyer?" Noah asked.

"No, definitely not," Abe said adamantly, not to scold his student, but to emphasize how important it is to let the buyer feel secure in the final price being offered. "If you just lower your price, it sends signals to the buyer that we've discussed. The buyer wonders if they could have done better still than the slight discount you offer. They wonder why you tried to sneak in extra profit in the first place. No, there are a lot of implications to actually benefit the buyer that should be considered in a negotiation. Make sense?"

Noah nodded.

"The wise thing to do is ask for a conditional commitment from the buyer to give you something in exchange for a better price. I call it 'get to give.' Seek low-cost concessions from the buyer that provides tangible value to you. Perhaps you could bulk a two-shipment order into one. Maybe the buyer will handle some of the service aspects that would normally cost you time and money. Consider asking for a commitment to additional purchases or extra products on the sale. Make sense?"

Noah nodded again, "In the end, it actually does save us money as a supplier to get those concessions and still really helps the buyer save money, right?"

Abe smiled and said, "Who am I to disagree with my own suggestion? So try it and see if it works for you. But know this...You should ask *conditionally* for the concession prior to making the offer. In other words, don't just say, 'I'll lower my price if you'll give me X.' Get X first. Instead ask, 'If I could work with my manager and company to lower the price a little, would you consider providing X as a concession I can take back to them?'

"Believe it or not," Abe continued, "it is a vital way to help your client save face and you, too. It's a legitimate request at bartering. If you simply offer a concession, the negotiation can go on with the buyer asking for more. Got it?"

Noah had been writing notes and looked up with soft intensity and said, "Got it."

The Get to Give Negotiation

Situation: The salesperson feels there is justification for a lower price

Strategy: Get to Give

Tactic: Ask for a low-cost concession that provides tangible return value

Key Concessions:
- Delivery – e.g., Pick-up, Flexibility, Bulk Deliveries
- Service – e.g., Enhanced Payment Terms, Transfer Administrative Duties
- Volume – e.g., Promise/Contract for More Volume
- Cross-Selling – e.g., Commitment to Additional Products Purchases

Figure 5.1

Does the list of concessions in Figure 5.1 look familiar? It should because they're the same issues a salesperson should discover to slow down the buying process as described in the bid avoidance presentation earlier, and are the same negotiation compromises to consider when the buyer asks for a lower price. A skilled sales negotiator knows that the best way to justify *giving* a concession is to *get* something in return.

Negotiate to Win-Win

You have been exposed to two strategies for getting your price. One strategy is to hold firm and accept your fate, the only true way to eventually get your original asking price. The other strategy offers insights into bartering that enable you to justify a slightly lower price while gaining something in return. The barter also defines for the buyer their responsibility to earn lower prices and ultimately creates the ideal win-win situation of compromise that defines solid relationships.

In the end, one key lesson of behavioral sales economics is to establish a pricing model that is based less on accidents and opinions and more on strategic insights and intentional tactical planning. Your first objective in the negotiation is to slow the sales dialogue early in the process. Your next step is to conduct discovery that enables you to put forth your best offer. Your final salvo in the price negotiation, if you can't get your asking price, is to plan a "get to give" compromise that creates a win-win relationship.

6

The Chess Game of Selling

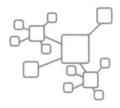

Success Is Situational Application

Malcolm Gladwell asserted in *Outliers* that it takes ten thousand hours to become an expert in your field. His work has popularized the concept of those ten thousand hours, although he didn't really prove it was exactly that many, nor how expertise is achieved except that it takes practice. He supports his thesis with anecdotal stories about the Beatles, professional hockey players, and other successful performers. They share the common experience of practice, lots of it in fact. Gladwell's thesis nevertheless is dubious and I can prove it.

Ask any hack golfer, a club to which I belong. My father introduced me to golf at the ripe old age of eleven and I have been playing with family members, friends, and business associates ever since. By conservative calculations, I've accumulated over twenty thousand hours of practice and I am still a hack golfer, thus proving it is not enough to repeatedly engage in a task for thousands of hours…if the wrong skills are being practiced. *Outliers* is a good read and it turns out Gladwell isn't really wrong, but maybe more like incomplete; peak performance takes a lot of practice, but it can't be random.

In a truly groundbreaking book, *Peak*, Anders Ericsson describes his years of research studying and interviewing world-class musicians, athletes, and other peak performers. He agrees that it takes thousands of hours to become proficient at a task, but practice alone is not enough. The performer can't simply go through the motions, but instead must master a process with purposeful focus.

Among the many stories of his research, one of the more profound is the study of blindfold chess. Ericsson cites the story of the late Alexander Alekhine, one of the greatest chess players of all time, perhaps second only to Bobby Fischer, the famous American chess star of the 1970s. Chess players know Alekhine for his remarkable aggression and numerous eponymous strategies. The question to ask is whether Fischer, Alekhine, and others learned to become master chess players or were born with the natural gift of chess magic. Ericsson's book describes a famous feat in 1924 when Alekhine took on twenty-six opponents in a display of blindfold chess. This means that Alekhine sat at a table without being able to view the chessboards that each individual opponent could see while a facilitator called out the moves to Alekhine.

The chess board is laid out in an 8 x 8 grid, coded by columns from A to H and rows 1 to 8…that is if you're sitting on the white side of the table. If you're playing the black pieces, you have to memorize the board in reverse order, which is H to A and 8 to 1. So the facilitator might say, "Table 9. Pawn D4," meaning the pawn moves to D4. A moment later the facilitator might say, "Table 17. Rook B7." And so on. Alekhine eventually won sixteen games, lost five, and played to a draw in five others over a period of ten hours during which he memorized the location of 832 chess pieces on 1,664 squares.

It is remarkable enough that any chess player could remember the location of the pieces and just *play* the games, let alone win with consistency. If you're at all like me, you have walked through a parking lot pressing your key fob hoping to hear the beep of the missing car you parked only moments earlier!

Ericsson describes a clever test created by his mentor, Herb Simon, to assess the memorization abilities of chess players at all skill levels where a grand master is rated above 2,500 and an amateur is below 900. Each player was given a brief, five-second view of a chess game in progress. You can take the test, too; it's fun! Observe the chessboard in Figure 6.1 and allow yourself five seconds to memorize the pieces of the board.

Figure 6.1

Not surprisingly, the higher the rank, the more the chess player could remember. Master level chess players would remember the location of nearly every piece observed on the chessboard in Figure 6.1 while you likely struggled. The player with expertise will also "be able to reproduce the most important areas of the board almost perfectly." No surprise there.

Players were next shown a random assortment of chess pieces on a board. Give yourself another five seconds to view the board in Figure 6.2 and see how well you do. If you did as poorly on the second test as the first, don't feel badly. Alekhine and Fischer would not fare better, nor would any other grand master when given views of the second chessboard. It is because the random assortment of pieces in Figure 6.2 is not a game in progress. It provides no strategic context that skilled chess players would recognize to remember the board layout. This study proved that chess expertise is not a matter of natural talent or visual acuity. It is a skill that is learned.

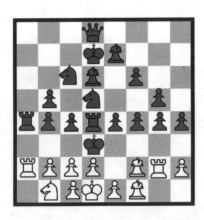

Figure 6.2

Grand masters are experts not because of natural talent at birth, but because over many years they have memorized up to fifty thousand situations likely to arise at some point on the chessboard. They have prepared strategies and tactics that best address each *situation*. In another study of verbal memory, you can ask someone to recall a random assortment of words—"life turn could fast around jockeys the dear whipped the it amazing was for horses so the hold on"— and they will remember up to the first few words only. If you provide the same words in the context of a sentence—"the horses whipped around the turn so fast it was amazing the jockeys could hold on for dear life"—most people will remember most of the words and some will remember them all. The difference is *context*.

There is a lot about these studies and Ericsson's larger work that we can apply to the profession of selling. A salesperson encounters a career of interactions with clients and prospects that provide strategic opportunities to apply game theory. For each situation, there is an evaluation to make and corresponding strategies and tactics to employ. The longer a salesperson lasts in the profession, the more insights and skills they gain, right? Wrong.

We've already proven that you can be a hack golfer for decades if you are not dedicated to constant improvement. Expertise requires more than activity; it requires the conscious study of situationally applied skills. A salesperson who executes a mediocre year of performance repeatedly over a twenty-year career is not as skilled as one who grows and improves every year. The blight of sales careers is the false belief that there is nothing new to learn in the profession of selling; experts never stop growing and realize the profession itself is evolving. Stay relevant or be left behind.

I'm Okay but You're Not

A study conducted by my company, Building Leaders, Inc., revealed that the opinions salespeople have of their performance versus other salespeople differ greatly. Salespeople were asked to rate their performance and an astounding 71% rated themselves as above average or excellent while less than 10% rated themselves as below average or poor. Conversely, the same respondents agreed that most salespeople hover pretty close to average. In fact, by definition the typical salesperson's performance *is* average.

Figure 6.3 illustrates the gap between actual performance and self-perceptions. Lots of salespeople think they are bringing up the curve, but few believe they are bringing it down. It's like a variation on the old self-help book, *I'm OK—You're OK.* In this case, the book is, *I'm OK, but Wow Do You Have Problems.* So why the gap?

First, positive results enable salespeople and managers to assume successful performance has occurred by measure of results. As we've already proven, a lot of salespeople in the business-to-business world enjoy high levels of transactional dependability in spite of deficient performance. Sales results are an obstacle for skill development not only for the performer, but for leaders as well. If orders are streaming consistently and results are the only measure of competence, there is no evidence to support change.

The Gap Between Actual and Perceived Skills

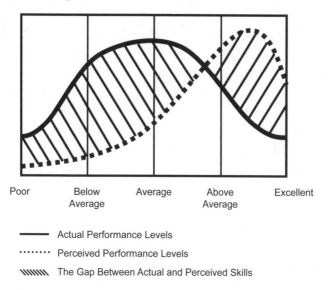

| Poor | Below Average | Average | Above Average | Excellent |

———— Actual Performance Levels

•••••••• Perceived Performance Levels

\\\\\\ The Gap Between Actual and Perceived Skills

Figure 6.3: Of salespeople surveyed, 71% rated themselves above average or excellent. Over 90% rated themselves average or better. The bell curve representing the law of averages indicates the actual skill levels of salespeople. The "gap" is the difference between actual performance and perceived levels. Salespeople, in other words, commonly believe they are bringing up the average and rarely the ones bringing it down.

Second, selling is a profession that requires a degree of self-esteem and persistence. Confidence and belief in one's own ability is essential. However, 49.99% of all salespeople are below average and over 80% of them, according to my study, deny they are part of that category. The goal here is to learn objectively what produces predictable outcomes without destroying the valuable self-confidence necessary for success. Blind faith in one's own performance and a lack of willingness to learn present obstacles to personal growth.

Third, selling is not a perfect science and therefore makes it easy for salespeople to rationalize unproven opinions. For example, a salesperson might attempt the bid avoidance presentation or the get to give negotiation strategy and fail to get desired results. It would be easy for a salesperson to quickly assert that the tactics don't work. This, however, would be as naïve as a professional baseball player arguing that the best pitch to hit is a curveball way out of the strike zone because there was "that one time when it worked."

A baseball player looks for optimum opportunities of waist-high fastballs because those are the best percentage opportunities even if it means missing some of the time. A truly skilled sales leader recognizes that there is a predictability about outcomes for each action. The goal is not guaranteed success, but improvement of percentages.

Selling Is a Process

Selling is a process. There are predictable outcomes to be objectively measured based on behaviors executed by different salespeople. Behavioral sales economics pursues an unbiased definition of superior performance. At some point, the words and actions learned become rote and the sales dialogue of the expert evolves and sounds less rehearsed over time to become strategically conversational. The salesperson can argue selling is a matter of style and it is true that a performer can bring their style to the process. That being said, process comes first.

For this reason, the bid avoidance presentation is delivered as both Abe's script and as an outline. The outline is the process; this script is Abe's (or my) voice. The process should be evaluated by salespeople using the same content. Consistent performance enables consistent evaluation and reveals opportunities for performance improvement. Salespeople can use their own vocabulary, inflections, and gestures to introduce personal style, but the content of reasoning for the meeting must be tested and proved—i.e., *proper pricing requires knowledge of delivery, service, volume, and the total mix of product opportunity.*

Process comes before style. Salespeople who shun "canned" presentations and sales strategies are making an error in professional judgment. Strategies and tactics that work in one situation should be tested repeatedly and used as long as they are effective or can be replaced with superior strategies and tactics.

Trial and Observation

This leads us to the quintessential skill of behavioral sales economics—*trial and observation.* The terminology is a variation on the popular concept of "trial and error" because it is a necessarily different approach to sales behavior and analysis. Unlike the useful process of trial and error in the practice of scientific exploration, trial and observation takes into account the unpredictability of human behavior.

Trial and error works in the sciences such as physics, chemical reactions, and biology because a stimulus that causes a change once predicts guaranteed outcomes in the future. In human behavior, such as sales activity, the stimulus that works in one situation may not always work in another. The goal is to evaluate the percentages.

Therefore, when Abe told Noah that the bid avoidance presentation worked every time, it was not because the outcomes were predictable, but instead because there *was* an outcome to analyze. If the buyer agreed to the meeting, the bid avoidance presentation advanced the sale; if not, it revealed concerning information about the potential opportunity. Either way, the presentation successfully helps the performer learn and grow closer to peak performance.

Abe and Noah can take the time, if they are inclined, to analyze how frequently the bid avoidance strategy gains an appointment and how often not. Suppose the strategy works three times out of ten, thus providing a 30% success ratio. The sales team of Abe and Noah can now test other sales behaviors and determine if there is a better way. If an alternative action produces a 40% success ratio, then clearly it is a superior tactic; if not, then the bid avoidance strategy will continue to be the optimum performance approach.

In this way, even a single sentence or question can be tested for effectiveness. This is the power of behavioral sales economics. As an example, I have told many times the story of the car salesman who asked when I walked into his dealership, "What changed in your life that brought you into the showroom today?" It's a question that Chuck Mann asked all of his customers, because it works!

The question enables Chuck to open the hearts of his customers while, at the same time, generating the exact information he needs to discuss car-buying options. In my case, I had accepted a new job and would be giving up a company car. He used that information to ask me more about the job, how I would use the car, and if I were willing to define the car allowance I had been offered by my new employer. I happily shared it all with him and bought a car.

Decide for yourself if you like Chuck's question or not, but recognize that the quality of the question should be analyzed as a matter of degree. It might not work 100% of the time, but it is certainly better than the alternatives such as "How can I help you today?" or "What's it going to take to get you behind the wheel tonight?"

The real power, therefore, of sales expertise and growth is the ability to objectively establish correlations between behaviors and outcomes. Consider that the bid avoidance presentation presumes that blind bids are an ineffective means to build sales traction. If, in fact, a blind bid to a buyer would yield a 50% closing ratio and no measureable improvement is created by an actual meeting, then the value of the bid avoidance presentation would be moot. This, however, is not the case.

The blind bid, for salespeople in business-to-business roles, has been measured to yield very low success rates, hovering near 5% in some industries. Twenty proposals requiring a few hours each to gain one sale is a lot of time. The bid avoidance presentation frees up time and accomplishes two outcomes. First, it enables the salesperson to selectively engage buyers with sincerity, thus raising closing ratios. Second, it frees up time that would be invested in paperwork and pricing with unqualified buyers to solicit better prospect opportunities elsewhere.

The real goal of trial and observation is to establish objective criteria for constant improvement to sales performance. This is the essence of behavioral sales economics, specifically to validate what Anders Ericsson proved in his groundbreaking book *Peak*.

A salesperson who has been at the job for thirty years cannot claim expertise merely by enduring. Success requires purposeful performance and the pursuit of personal growth. It requires trial and observation.

Proactive Consciousness

Behavioral sales economics is the practice of developing the right behaviors. It means identifying the common situations you will face, establishing a strategy, and then taking the right actions. A few examples have been provided. Buyers who wish to speed up the process (*situation*) should be slowed down (*strategy*) with the bid avoidance presentation (*tactic*). Buyers who pressure for lower prices (*situation*) should give to get (*strategy*) with specific concessions identified before the negotiation begins (*tactic*). Cold prospects walking into a dealership (*situation*) should be encouraged to first discuss their situation (*strategy*) with a question such as, "What has changed in your life…" (*tactic*).

There remains a missing link—predictability. The strategies and tactics are only useful if they produce desired results. This means that a serious student of the profession is proactively and consciously evaluating the outcomes of their actions.

Let's consider one common situation that occurs millions of times each year—a walk-in customer. The most common question asked is, "Can I help you?" This question is met reflexively with the same answer 90% of the time, specifically, "No, thanks. Just looking." If the salesperson really were interested in helping the buyer or pursuing a better dialogue, new questions should be tested. Chuck Mann offered one by asking, "What changed in your life…?"

I have tested with clients the question, "What is it going to take to get you out of here today?" Imagine you just walked into a lumberyard and the sales associate greeted you with that question. We discussed and believed it could be delivered with humor and just enough shock value to elicit a response. Thus we tested it and measured the outcome.

Typically the conversation at that point takes off. Consistently we found that people responded with the answer, "You want to get me out of here?" Naturally the seller isn't really trying to get the buyer out of the store, but recognizes that there *is* a reason the buyer is in it and, more importantly, probably does *not* want to spend the entire day at the lumberyard. The question creates more engagement than, "Can I help you?" That is the purpose of trial and observation.

The first responses you have to various situations might not be optimal. However, if you at least recognize both common and unique situations as they arise, you will be equipped to consciously test responses and improve them over time. The chess game of selling is one in which you consistently observe situations and build your arsenal of strategies and tactics through the process of trial, observation…and then proactive consciousness.

We have already established that many salespeople can achieve lofty results by accident. The process of trial and observation enables all salespeople and managers to look objectively at facts, behaviors, and events to achieve success on purpose. The analysis, however, is incomplete until the performer, perhaps working with a mentor or colleague, considers the outcomes of a performance after the fact.

Proactive consciousness is the, after the fact, *calm process of replaying experiences that occurred in the heat of the moment as the means to develop lessons and practices for future similar situations*—i.e., trial, observation, *and (now) repetition*. Proactive consciousness is a vital skill for the process of achieving success *on purpose*. Unlike Eastern spirituality that teaches us to live in the present, this is an intentional look backwards without regret or judgment. It is an evaluation that can improve future performance.

Tyler was a salesman who contacted me for advice about a potential client with whom he had never worked. The bid avoidance presentation failed and he asked me what I would do.

"I would pass," I told him. "But the real question is: What are *you* going to do?"

Not surprisingly, the eager young salesman wanted to go for any opportunity no matter how small the chances for success. He decided he was going to give the buyer a price to which I made two suggestions. The first was that he tell the buyer up front he is going to provide a price on the condition that the buyer allow Tyler to present his proposal when it was ready. The second is that he pay close attention to the outcome of the process.

Two days later Tyler called me to say the buyer wouldn't meet, but still demanded the price that required two hours of preparation. Tyler asked me what I would do in that situation. I assured him I would hold onto my work until a time when the prospect was willing to engage in conversation, but that Tyler should do what he feels best on the condition, again, that he pay close attention to the outcome of his actions.

My experience of trial, observation, and proactive consciousness has taught me over the years that buyers, having no investment in *their* time with me, feel little obligation to honor *mine*. The result consistently has been buyers who quickly assure me my prices were not competitive. Predictably, Tyler delivered the price and was told his it was too high. Two hours of Tyler's life were dismissed in a matter of seconds by an uninvolved buyer.

A few weeks later, Tyler called and told me a buyer wanted his price, but refused to meet even after the bid avoidance presentation. At that point, I asked Tyler to practice his bid avoidance approach with me and it sounded very good. In fact, he verified that it had worked numerous times for him. He asked me again what I would do. Again, I turned the question back to him while assuring him that he already knew what I would do.

Tyler spoke music to my ears when he said, "I see this as a bad lead. I really want to pass, but thought I'd run it by you."

You can already guess what my pleased response was to him.

This is how *proactive consciousness* works. It's not enough to act. The skilled sales leader, or peak performer in any endeavor, takes the extra time to analyze as the primary means for constant performance improvement.

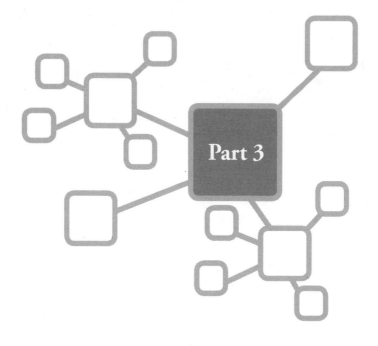

KPIs and KRIs

7

KPIs: The Success In-Between

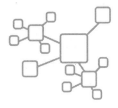

Success Is In the In-Between

My weight loss plan was succeeding even if my weight was *rising*! Three weeks after making the momentous decision to shed twenty pounds, I realized my scale was defective. After all, I *had* made the decision to succeed. That's how the pursuit of a goal starts. You make a decision and a commitment to succeed...and then the plan comes to a screeching halt.

As Robert Burns famously wrote, "The best laid plans of mice and men often go awry." Predictably, my scale was working perfectly well, but my plan was broken. I got the first part right, the decision to achieve a goal. I forgot the second, the commitment to the plan. It's kind of how sales goals work. The salesperson begins the year with enthusiasm and belief.

As the monthly results roll in, the salesperson realizes the numbers aren't adding up and the plan, or lack of it, is falling short of goals.

I did the thing many people do. I set a goal, established a deadline, and then waited. It wasn't so much procrastination as it was lacking a blueprint for success. The vague intent was to do some sensible eating and light exercise as change enough to produce desired results. Of course, I hadn't defined what "sensible" eating meant, nor established a measurable exercise plan. I changed, but not in the right way…or enough…or both!

I cut out bread, sort of. I rarely ate chocolate more than once per day, at least not more than twice hardly ever. Instead of ordering onion rings with the lunchtime cheeseburger, I switched to french fries. I continued joking that lettuce was nothing more than crunchy, unfulfilling water. I habitually went on late-night cereal binges and rationalized them because at least I chose Cheerios over my preferred Cap'n Crunch. Imagine my surprise when the pounds didn't melt away. In short, I was aware of the things I was eating after the fact, but not planning in advance what I should be eating…or not be.

As ridiculous as it sounds, there is not a falsehood in the story. I doubt I am alone. I had never weighed myself with any consistency until an unexpectedly large man was looking back at me in the mirror. Once I started weighing myself regularly, I didn't like the results. It's true that I had changed my eating habits slightly, albeit with no clear plan or measurement scheme. In a new version of the dictum on insanity where you foolishly do the same thing while expecting a different result, I actually did something *different* to get the *same* result. I didn't do the *right* different things or follow a plan. That is insanity.

It turns out success isn't about setting a goal and measuring results; it's about the work *in between* the goal and the outcome. Ask anyone who has successfully lost significant weight and you will consistently hear stories of behavioral changes performed habitually over long periods of time. Luck might get the result, but that's as repeatable as the child who can't show his work in pursuit of the math answer. Accidental success is not repeatable. Success on purpose means defining the habits and establishing necessary measurements that lead to desired outcomes. It means committing to measurement of the *in-between*.

The Power of the "In-Between"

Figure 7.1: The *in-between* is the commitment to change habits after deciding on a desired outcome and the measurement of actual results. The *in-between* is the period of time when performance activities are established and measured in pursuit of the outcome. The *in-between* evolves into more than a time period. It becomes the "proving ground" to validate the correlations between performance and outcomes.

Figure 7.1 illustrates the success process for a dieter, starting with a goal for the future. Regular measurements of outcomes are valuable trackers of performance success, but meaningless without the actual performance in between. During this period, the dieter must establish behavioral objectives and measurements of actual performance designed to align with future goals. During the in-between, the performer periodically measures results to determine if the plan is working. If so, the plan continues; if not, the plan is adjusted.

Commitment Is In Between

Successful goal attainment is more than a short-term commitment to change as proven by the many people who have successfully lost weight only to later put it back on. Losing weight is not an event; it's a lifestyle change. Meaningful goals require meaningful change. The in-between is more than a time period. It's a change in lifestyle and even more. It's the development of permanent new habits.

The in-between is the process by which individuals and organizations become great. Consistent, quality performance is the key to business and personal success. Anyone can set a goal and fail. Millions of New Year's Eve resolutions that fail within the first few months are living proof. The optimism for the New Year is quickly diminished by the realization that a resolution is more than a sentence. It requires self-obligation to new habits and the discipline to measure those habits and resulting outcomes. The power of the in-between ultimately becomes more than the attainment of the goal; it is what individuals and organizations *become*.

The in-between provides salespeople with a process to *become* powerful, self-assured, and confident in their long-term professional security. It's the difference between job and career security. Job security is what is offered from an employer; career security is earned. This was the challenge my sales candidate was facing while looking for a new job. He wanted an offer that would provide another oasis for a paycheck based on transactional dependability. Job security is *external* to the performer because it can be taken away; career security is *internal* because it is based on the experience and confidence to know how to repeat success. The real power of weight loss is not just the result, but the gratification that comes from accomplishing an audacious goal intentionally. The same is true for salespeople who achieve lifelong career security with a process discovered during the in-between.

The in-between, for organizations, is how they *become* market brand leaders with sustainable reputations, contagious cultures, and unbreakable customer loyalty. It is the difference between accidental achievement of corporate goals and intentional, repeatable success. It is the plan by which organizations establish performance benchmarks, cultural values, and controlled outcomes that last. In *Good to Great*, Jim Collins made famous the concept of "Level 5 Leadership," the type of leadership that forgoes the pursuit of short-term results in favor of systematic process development designed to create long-term, lasting success.

Level 5 success is not about a slogan, personality, or temporary initiative. Level 5 success is sustainable because a defined program of excellence and correlation between performance measurements and results exists. Microsales provides the blueprint of individual performance to become repeatable by all sales team members as the means to make sales-driven organizations great.

The in-between breeds confidence not merely for achieving a one-time goal, but for developing the practices that make success repeatable. It is a test and observe "proving ground," the test laboratory in which a theory of accomplishment is planned, observed, and adjusted.

The Proving Ground

I joked that my weight-loss plan was failing due to a defective scale when of course it was the performer or, more aptly described, a defective *performance*. The good news is that I didn't wait for months to measure my weight, but had started a daily practice. This habit proved that the plan wasn't working and revisions needed to be made. It proved I needed to take responsibility for my own performance, a critical flaw for many in their game plan that starts during a late-night commercial.

The television ad promises easy weight loss to inspire an unhappy viewer munching on a bag of Cheetos to take action. The tear-jerking images of miracle case weight loss studies motivate the viewer to know they can be one of those success stories. The only necessary commitment is to make the first of four easy payments and start the journey toward fitness. The inspired viewer buys the plan and devolves into old habits quickly, presuming they ever took action in the first place. They soon quit the plan, usually before the last payment is made. The problem for the dieter is not lack of desire or intention.

The problem is the lack of in-between commitment. The dieter observed only the before and after, not the in-between, thus inspiring enough enthusiasm to make the purchase. If the commercial, based on historical data, issued a warning of likely of failure, it would be a more honest commercial but hardly a successful sales campaign. If the commercial had illustrated the necessary commitment in between to stick with the plan for weeks, months, and years, the viewer would logically analyze and rethink the purchase while losing the emotional impulse to buy. The commercial omitted the story of the in-between because it's bad salesmanship.

The ads are so clever that, in fact, they offer testimonials from dieters that "never had to give up the foods they love." The reality of dieting is that you *do* sacrifice during the in-between. You give up foods you love. You commit to an exercise regimen. Then you adjust for the challenges that are unique to your body and lifestyle. In short, successful goal achievement requires the performer to take responsibility for the in-between.

Some individuals give up sugary sodas and candy while starting a consistent exercise regimen. Others find the reduction of carbohydrates and an increase in proteins is their key to success. For some, counting calories using one of the many apps on the market is enough to create new habits. Others join clubs that create point systems for food, which actually work for those who stick with the plans. If you want to succeed at any important endeavor you need to change *and measure* your habits. You need to define the key performance indicators (KPIs) of success.

Key performance indicators as a measurement term of business performance is nothing new. KPIs have been used to measure business competencies in a variety of categories including financial performance of a business, operational efficiencies, and sales predictability. KPIs are an inescapable truth of sales economics, at least for those who want to succeed on purpose. The problem, for the purposes of sales economics theory, is that the key performance indicators (KPIs) for *sales* have long been misunderstood.

KRIs Are Not KPIs

If you ask most executives, managers, and salespeople to define the KPIs of sales success, they commonly emphasize measurements including sales volume, profit margins, sales comparisons to previous year totals, and other topline data. The problem is that these KPIs are not *leading* indicators. Profits, margins, and other sales results are better defined as KRIs, or key results indicators. KRIs are *lagging* indicators resulting from the proper execution of measured performance.

KPIs Come First

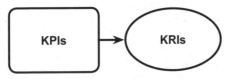

Figure 7.2: KRIs are the outcomes desired, but unmanageable until the proper performance benchmarks are established and performed. Sales economics for microsales and macrosales establishes the key performance indicators (KPIs) that lead to predictable results.

Performance creates results, not the other way around. You can't manage results, but you can manage performance. Thus, as illustrated in Figure 7.2, KPIs must come *before* KRIs. Weight loss is the desired result—i.e., the *key result indicator (KRI)*; diet and exercise are the *key performance indicators* to measure in pursuit of the result—i.e., the *KPIs*. One set of data (KPIs) is predictive while the other category (KRIs) provides indicators of performance success or failure. Manage and measure to the right performance metrics and the results will follow. If you ignore the performance measurements, results are a matter of luck.

In sales, the KRIs of volume, profits, year-to-date comparisons, and other results-based measurements are certainly vital benchmarks of performance success, but not predictors of success.

KPIs Are "In-Between"

Figure 7.3: Results are after-the-fact measurements to establish the quality of performance and performance metrics. If desired results are achieved (or in progress) then the plan is working and performance should become habitual. If results are not achieved, then performance must be adjusted to achieve the original desired outcomes.

Figure 7.3 illustrates the power of key performance indicators (KPIs), which influence business results in the same way they influence weight loss, except for one glaring problem. Defining the correct sales KPIs has historically been a murky process at best and an undefined one at worst. Is it possible to quantify the value of a sales call when no sale occurs? What KPIs lead to short-term transactional success? What metrics can be ascribed to the value of a relationship? What KPIs should be measured to predict long-term sales success? How can performance metrics enable an individual or organization to achieve predictable results on purpose? In short, what are the KPIs of *sales* success?

Success is not a short-term event that suddenly happens in a moment of epiphany. Success is gradual and creeps up on you while you're busy sticking to a game plan. Success is the thing that happens before the results roll in and is directly linked to the prior performance whether measured or not. Sales economics is about measuring the performance *in-between*. It begins with a scorecard of success that the performer uses to build a career.

8

The Scorecard
of Your Career

A Game of Honor

In the 1925 U.S. Open, Bobby Jones performed the act that creates legends. Jones is famously known as one of the greatest golfers of all time, and also the founder of Augusta National Golf Club and the Masters Tournament. All those credentials aside, it wasn't a feat of golf on June 3, 1925, at the Worcester Golf Club in Massachusetts that added to Jones's legend. It was an act of honor that established his reputation and influenced the game of golf for decades to come.

On the eleventh hole of the U.S. Open Golf Championship, Jones lined up his iron shot and noticed his ball move slightly after he had "addressed" it, technically a violation of the rules even if the player's club never makes contact with the ball. Jones eyed the movement and called a penalty on himself even though it had gone unnoticed by anyone else. Several observers suggested he had made a mistake. They tried talking him out of the self-assessed penalty, but Jones was having none of it. He was sure of himself and took the one stroke penalty, which contributed to an eventual tie at the tournament's end, thus forcing an eighteen-hole playoff. He lost.

It was a matter-of-fact decision Jones put into perspective when deflecting the abundant praise later heaped on him. "You might as well praise me for not robbing a bank," Jones stated simply. His honor set the tone for the game with a gesture that has been duplicated by other professionals following in his footsteps over many decades, many of whom lost golf tournaments and large purses as a result of their honesty.

In other sports, you push and bend the rules to gain whatever competitive advantage you can muster. In golf, part of the game's attraction is the fact that you play within the rules…and more. You enforce your own adherence to the regulations. To cheat the game is only to cheat yourself.

That's how the scorecards of sales economics work. Performers must track their own performances with honesty and accuracy. To cheat the sales scorecard is only to cheat yourself. To ignore it altogether is to leave yourself blindly hoping to succeed without a game plan. This was the very direction a former pupil was headed when I walked into his office.

It's Your Scorecard

Kent sat across the desk from me before we would leave for a day of sales calls in the field scheduled as a sales coaching session. I casually mentioned during our planning dialogue in his office that it had been a few weeks seen I had seen his "prospect tracker," the ongoing list and value of leads you create. He sheepishly admitted his needed to put in "updates" and promised he'd send his scorecard to me later.

"You don't have to promise me anything," I said without agenda or judgment. "It's your asset. I'm here to help if you ever need it. Just know that."

"I know. I know," he said with rising angst. "I have to get it to you."

"No," I said calmly. "You don't. It's your scorecard. It's for you to measure your performance. We've been through the discussion and I think you know what to do with it. If you send it, I can probably offer some tweaks and insights. But don't worry about me. I work for you. I'm a coach, just like your golf coach. You can practice the swing techniques… or not. You can track your activity…or not. It's for you. I'm available to help when you want."

Truth be told, his employer was funding my time and this probably made Kent feel guilty. As a means to save face, he sat back in his chair and asked if I wanted to hear a story about a great sales interaction from the previous day. He was displaying the habit I call a "deflection," the moment when a salesperson, or any performer for that matter, strives to shift the dialogue from an uncomfortable subject to a story of bravado and success. It is a method to avoid looking at the real scorecard of performance and a means to justify rating oneself as an above average or excellent performer without basis in fact.

"Sure!" I said with earnest interest. The ensuing fifteen-minute monologue was the old "so I say…then he says…which led me to…then I told him…at which point…" and so forth story. He emphasized the quality of the dialogue and beamed with pride as he described his sales acumen. Near the end of his epic tale, he leaned in to deliver the powerful punch line, "The meeting was a huge success and produced a candidate who might buy over $150,000 of our products."

Eureka! The real problem, and solution, hit me between the eyes!

"So," I asked, "You met a prospect yesterday who is sincerely interested in a potential relationship that we can value at $150,000, correct?"

"Yep," Kent said proudly, not taking or even recognizing the bait, but instead leaning back in his chair again.

"Huh. Interesting." Then I asked, "Did you put the information into your opportunity tracker?"

He groaned and admitted he had not, but still made no move to his computer to take action. Thus I suggested he take the time to enter the information while I waited.

"Like now?" he asked as if the administrative task would be some breach of time management protocol with his coach.

"Sure, why not?"

"I can," he said. "I just don't want to waste your time."

I smiled and assured him it would be no waste of my time and, in fact, the highest honor he could offer me. It would demonstrate his trust in my system of metrics and allow us the powerful opportunity to measure that in-between performance as a component of future results he might achieve. Finally, Kent got the hint and took the *one minute* necessary to enter the information. At that point, it was me leaning forward and staring at his monitor while he finished the task. After he completed the *one minute* exercise, I leaned back and with a deep sigh said, "Whew! You must be exhausted."

He chuckled and admitted it wasn't that hard to do and then heard me put the recent period of our mutual lives in perspective.

"We both know you run a great meeting," I said. "I've seen it and appreciate hearing your story. It took you fifteen minutes to tell me a story that I can recount in a few words, namely, 'You got a hot lead of $150,000!' That's the story. Enough said. It took you one minute to enter it into your opportunity tracker. Of the last fifteen minutes, which would you say were the most productive for you?"

Kent had to admit the data entry was far more beneficial to his success than the retelling of a story. That's when I decided we should talk about golf, a game at which we are both equally bad. We had golfed a few months earlier at an industry outing and shared a cart. I asked him if he remembered how we kept score, a non sequitur in his mind. "Um, yes," he said.

"How?" I asked.

"Um, by strokes, I guess. Is that what you mean?"

"Nope. I mean by hole. That's what I mean. You are correct that we count the strokes. I'm pointing out that we do it every hole." I then asked, "Did we wait until the last hole to look back and figure out what we scored on the previous eighteen or did we keep score one hole at a time?"

"Ahhh, got it," Kent said as the means to express a lesson learned and an understanding of the metaphor.

"What did you get from that?"

"Well…you're saying to keep score of every call I guess just like every hole, right?"

"Yep. That's it," I assured him before taking the conclusion to the next level. "What chance do you think you could recount the score you achieved on every hole if you wait for eighteen holes to keep score?"

Kent agreed there was no chance to get the numbers right if he waited.

"How much do you get paid to golf?" I asked.

Kent smiled because there was no need to answer.

"That's right," I said with a smile. "You and I wouldn't think for a second about teeing off on a hole until we've written down the score on the previous one…and golf doesn't even matter because it's not our job…and we stink at it! Yet, you have a scorecard in front of you that can create wealth and career security if you choose to use it. Which scorecard is more important—golf or the game of selling?"

"Selling," Kent said without a hint of defensiveness. He was a stellar student.

"The assets being offered to you are the scorecards of your career," I concluded. "Don't use them for me. Use them for you if you believe they will help. If so, then I can help you help yourself. End of lesson. Questions?"

"Nope."

"Think you might need to pay more attention to your scorecards?"

"Yep."

"Wanna hit the road and rack up some more scores?"

Kent smiled and said, "Let's do it!"

One Scorecard Is Not Enough

The analysis of sales performance is complex, just like measurements for any important endeavor. The scorecard in golf is simple and actually not a measurement of the KPIs, but instead an assemblage of KRIs in the form of individual golf scores that add up to the total value for a round of golf. The KPIs to measure include secondary data such as the number of putts, greens in regulation, up-and-downs from the bunker, and so forth. In baseball the KRIs are wins and losses; the KPIs include individual and team performance measurements for batting averages, on-base percentages, runs allowed, and more. The aforementioned "opportunity tracker" in selling is one of numerous KPI measurement scorecards available to help you measure the KPIs of the in-between that produce desired KRIs for monthly and annual sales goals.

Microsales and macrosales economics data provide insights and measurements for many different KPIs and KRIs that will be covered in the remainder of the book. The value of a sales call will be provided as both a KPI and KRI. The quality of that sales call will tie into the overarching measurement of calendar management, a vital indicator of sales competence. Sales campaigns will be analyzed as a "season" of performance where illustrations will provide measurements to attain long-term sales volume goals for salespeople working in environments of both high and low transactional dependability.

Throughout the book, aspects of behavioral sales economics will be introduced to offer more definitions of sales performance. This means understanding how subjective observations can lead to objective valuation of sales behavior. The quality of each individual observation and measurement will add up to a campaign of success. Not surprisingly, each category impacts the others.

The quality of a single sales interaction—e.g., phone call, email, or face-to-face meeting—will obviously impact long-term results as well as the KPI measurements of calendar management and the pursuit of long-term sales goals. A section will define the sales behaviors and information gathering that leads to strong relationships and therefore better results. Better relationships improve the objective quality of sales. Better sales calls vice versa improve the quality of relationships. The KPI of better sales calls leads to better calendar management by producing good weeks and months of performance leading to time management efficiency. And so on.

Admittedly the journey into microsales and macrosales economics will not be entirely linear, although it converges on a thesis and measurements that produce the singular outcome of better overall performance. The golfer breaks down larger processes into strategic skill development of driving, chipping, putting, and more. The chess player breaks down the process into offensive and defensive strategies for stages of chess identified as the opening, middle, and endgame. The performances of small skill sets become a sum of the parts for the overall performance.

In this way, the salesperson becomes a credible leader who achieves more confidence, stronger purpose, improved sales results, and ultimately the career security that emanates from extraordinary competence.

9

The Appointment as KRI and KPI

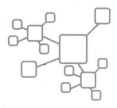

Statement of the Problems

Pop quiz!

On average, a scheduled meeting with a client will produce better outcomes than a cold call or pop-in visit. True or false?

The question, some would argue, is a foolish test of common sense. It seems obvious the answer is true—a scheduled appointment yields better outcomes *on average* than unscheduled visits if for no other reason than the fact that the potential buyer might not be present when the salesperson makes the pop-in. Appointments are such a vital aspect of sales performance excellence that they merit their own chapter of instruction.

Appointments with a defined purpose are a symbol or professionalism, predictors of productivity, and the vital component of sales success. It would seem unnecessary to even validate the power of a scheduled meeting over a cold call, yet many salespeople unfortunately choose to ignore the obvious, most notably salespeople in roles of high transactional dependability. As the saying goes, "Common sense is not common practice." Several case studies illustrate this lack of common sense.

CASE STUDY 1:
The Unwinnable Argument of Self-Delusion

The vice president for a manufacturer asked me, "What is the one thing, and most important thing, you believe our salespeople should take away from your training session today?" Without hesitation I strongly advised, based on my extensive experience working with *his* customer base, the sales reps should make appointments to differentiate themselves. His competitors and most salespeople in the manufacturer sales rep role rely on cold calls to fill their calendars, a habit clients find annoying.

One of his veteran salespeople instantly piped in to disagree. He asserted that he regularly drove his sales route without scheduling appointments because his customers "counted on him to pop in according to his usual schedule." He actually used the word "route," not realizing that, for some, he was relegating himself to a level of professionalism reserved for the paperboy delivering daily newspapers on a bicycle. He said, "Your advice is good for others, but I think my situation is different. My customers appreciate me stopping in."

I replied, "That's what most manufacturer sales reps say."

He replied with the utmost confidence, "I bet they do and probably believe it. In my case, it happens to be true."

I replied, "They say that, too."

He said, "But you don't know my customers and my relationships. I can tell just from the responses I get how much they appreciate my service. I have specific stops I make for each day during my two-week cycles."

"Interesting," I conceded. "It makes sense." There was no sense arguing with the salesman. He was self-assured and the transactional dependability of his role enabled him to believe what he wanted, although his performance as a route driver and commitment to his process seems good news for his competitors. He essentially was rating himself as an excellent salesperson even though his performance was the type frequently criticized behind his back by customers.

CASE STUDY 2:
"Tuesday" Does Not Define a Purpose

John was a manufacturer sales representative for a client. During a morning of work with John making calls to client offices, we made three stops where no appointment had been scheduled. The dialogues were brief and contained more personal chitchat than substantive business dialogue. For our fourth stop of the day, we pulled into the parking lot of one of his customers. Before allowing time for him or I to touch the door handles to open our doors, I asked, "What is the goal for your meeting here today?"

He said, "It's Tuesday."

"Got it. Very familiar with all the days," I said to mingle a little levity with coaching. "So, what's our goal? Maybe I can help."

John explained that he always visited this particular client every Tuesday. "They expect me," he concluded.

It was believable because, through the storefront window of the business, I could see three sales associates in a heated dialogue of gestures that seemed to translate into, "Oh boy. John is here. You deal with him because I had to last time." One associate threw her hands in the air and walked to the back warehouse before we entered. The other got on the phone, leaving the unfortunate third soul forced to accept John's cold call interruption.

"Anything you need from me today?" John asked.

The contact we met, Kerry, was a salesperson for the company. He shook my hand and told me he had attended one of my past seminars. After exchanging pleasantries, I answered a few questions Kerry had about my industry perspective. Then Kerry told John, "Everything is good. We're all set here today." Kerry added that he appreciated the visit, with finality, to imply the meeting was over. John didn't catch the hint even though Kerry never invited us past the retail sales counter and into his office to sit. John tried to keep the meeting alive by mentioning a new product that was coming out. Kerry assured John he had seen it at their local show.

John asked Kerry if there were any leads he needed help selling. Kerry smiled and said, "I was hoping you would bring me a lead." Kerry mentioned that he had placed three significant orders the week before to John's company. John thanked him for the business, made some additional small talk about recent sporting events, and departed with the promise to "see you next Tuesday."

His sales call documentation in the company CRM (customer relationship management) software was, like mine of years past, a creative writing assignment of bravado and productivity. After the meeting with Kerry, John could easily describe an enthusiastic reception for the new product he mentioned. He could embellish that aspect of the dialogue while also take credit for the recent orders even though he had not created nor influenced them in any tangible way. His manager wouldn't know John's actual performance unless he watched it. Simply reading the creative writing assignments traditionally called "sales call reports" is not enough.

It's one of the faults of our computer age that salespeople and managers presume the electronics of communication, in this case CRM software, will enhance productivity and communication. The obligation John felt for "reporting to the boss" with the software was identical to the handwritten call reports of his past. The electronic process is still a creative writing assignment. And "Tuesday" is still not a solid purpose for a cold call.

CASE STUDY 3:
The Jury of One Is Still Deliberating

Matt is a salesperson for another manufacturer I worked with. He is also a great guy to share a beer with, but not golf. Matt is a two handicap, meaning he was very, *very* good at golf. He practices his golf game five times per week.

In the days before GPS, I sat shotgun in his truck and navigated directions to the meeting at his prospect's office.

The forty-five minute drive seemed excessive, but well-timed to arrive at the noon hour.

"Are we going to lunch?" I asked.

"No. Just a cold call. They don't know we're coming."

I suggested to Matt that it might have been better to phone ahead because staff members would be on lunch break and a cold call interruption might not be welcomed if they were short-staffed. He assured me that "this is a company where it's okay to make the cold call." Then fate lent a hand to deliver a sales lesson that was soon revealed in a manner too ironic to be considered anything other than divine intervention.

We arrived just past the noon hour, asked the receptionist for the location manager, and waited. The manager came to greet us and enthusiastically said he wanted to learn more about Matt's products, but it had to be another time. "You've caught us doing inventory today and we're short. I can't talk now, but I'm definitely interested to hear what you have to offer. Let's set something up in the future."

As a natural reflex to avoid embarrassment in front of an observing coach, Matt tried to lengthen the conversation. He pushed to get a few minutes of presentation time to no avail. We had driven fifty minutes out of our way, one way. Matt didn't even attempt to suggest a future date and time for the meeting that, moments earlier, the prospect actually requested!

The most noteworthy lesson was the incredible denial of common sense in favor of self-justification. On the drive to our next meeting, I asked Matt if he agreed that an appointment would have been more productive than a cold call for the last stop. Shockingly he said, "The jury it still out on that."

At the end of the day, during the feedback portion of our coaching session, I suggested to Matt that he could be one of the greatest salespeople of all time if he put half as much energy into his sales development as he put into his golf game. He said he would think about that idea while I silently concluded his performance was being poorly judged by a jury of one. Matt's territory sales were steady because he worked for a highly regarded manufacturer of products, thus enabling him to defer or deny completely any self-examination of his skills; Kahneman called it "the illusion of skill." Maybe it would be better noted as the self-delusion of skill.

The Rest of the Story

A famous radio personality named Paul Harvey had a syndicated audience of millions for over half a century. He would regale his audience by spinning a human interest or historic tale before cutting to the sponsorship announcements. After the advertisements, Harvey came back on to the radio to offer a twist by famously saying, "And now, the rest of the story…"

In the spirit of this radio legend, here is the "rest of the story on appointments…"

The story on appointments is the *buyer's perspective*, something I have been lucky enough to gain by observing salespeople. Many clients of mine are resellers of goods purchased from a manufacturer. Therefore I've been able to gain a perspective as the shopper frequently interacting with manufacturer sales representatives. To be fair and clear, the goal is *not* to indict manufacture sales representatives. The objective is to illustrate for the salespeople, from a buyer's perspective, how annoying a cold call can be to a customer if it is conducted improperly.

Cold call interruptions are not the exclusive domain of any single category of salesperson or industry. They are a crutch that enables salespeople to substitute accomplishment with nonproductive activity. It's not "manufacturer representatives" as a category; it's ineffective salespeople...regardless of the product or sales category.

The Appointment as KRI

Three case studies illustrate a level of denial and rationalization that is surprising and raises questions. Why did they defend behavior that is so obviously deficient? How could they not see unscheduled pop-ins as anything other than interruptions to their clients? What incentive is there to justify inferior performance? The short answer is that cold calls, in spite of the annoyance to clients and ineffectiveness, are a byproduct of transactional dependability. If the orders are coming in, what reason is there for self-reflection and change?

Appointments take work and, more importantly, a level of skill that many salespeople have not developed. An appointment is the key results indicator (KRI) of the salesperson's abilities. It is a *lagging* indicator that measures multiple facets of skills including sales prospecting, account management, time management, and consultative selling.

The appointment is also a *measure of persistence* because no salesperson can successfully get an appointment with 100% success. Considering that the appointment might require numerous phone calls, emails and even pop-in visits, it clearly indicates the appointment is a factor of persistence. Rejection is part of the job.

In *The Pursuit of Happyness*, Will Smith plays the role of Chris Gardner, a homeless father struggling to raise his son while launching a career as a stockbroker. Smith's character describes how he could save time and make more calls per day by pressing the button to hang up his phone while keeping the receiver close to his ear. The movie may have taken some cinematic license on this subject (although I suspect that particular detail was gleaned from Mr. Gardner himself and is likely true). Anyone who has ever sold securities, as I did for two years, will tell you one thing is certain regardless of how you hang up the phone and begin the next call: you have to be a cold-calling machine willing to accept constant rejection.

Gardner runs the numbers and calculates how many calls it takes just to make contact. Keeping them on the phone after the first sentence is an essential skill in securities sales, because most people hang up immediately. Assuming you can make it that far, it might take five conversations out of the original one hundred dials to set an actual appointment. The appointment for a stockbroker is a powerful KRI for the KPIs of persistence calculated as the number of calls required for each scheduled appointment. Even if salespeople in other professions can take it for granted, they shouldn't.

The Appointment as a Key RESULTS Indicator

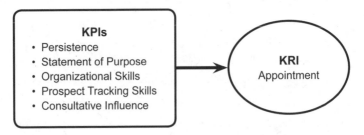

Figure 9.1: An appointment is a demonstration of quality skills and a key results indicator of performance success. An appointment proves the level of persistence necessary to overcome rejection in the sales profession. It illustrates the performer has delivered the right message with a purpose that suits the buyer's needs. It infers the organizational skills for time management, customer record keeping, and calendar management. It requires detailed prospect tracking to follow up on leads when success is not achieved on the first try. In short, the appointment is a lagging indicator that proves sales competence on many levels.

Figure 9.1 illustrates the correlation between the KPIs of scheduling appointments, in this case the KRI. The KPI is the *leading indicator* of future success while the KRI is the *lagging indicator* of a job well performed. The ability to schedule appointments is a KRI of the salesperson's ability to craft *the right script* for a phone call or pop-in visit; a valuable *statement of purpose* that inspires the buyer; persistence to press on in the face of adversity; the *ability to document and track data* for follow-up dialogues; and the *ability to influence* positively.

Cold Calls Count for Something

To be clear, there is nothing wrong with a cold call. In fact, it is a core skill to master for salespeople seeking high levels of success in their careers. For this reason, I have always valued the pop-in visit as a legitimate use of time if certain caveats are met.

First, a cold call that could have been executed more effectively over the phone, rather than a fifty-minute drive, is a superior use of time. A cold call that is made as a fill-in stop during the day, provided it doesn't take a salesperson out of the planned route, is also effective. Cold calls have their place and the most effective way to conduct a *lot* of them is over the phone, with a purpose.

Second, the only legitimate *purpose* a salesperson should expect from a cold call is to schedule a future meeting. In this day and age of distractions and hyper stimulation, it is unrealistic to expect meaningful dialogues when not scheduled in advance. Of course, on occasion, that the prospect will welcome a dialogue during a cold call, but proper courtesy is to not expect it.

If the salesperson lucks out and catches the buyer at a fortunate moment, it's time to ring the bell and recognize that the remainder of the dialogue is actually an "appointment" created during the walk-in cold call. The caution here for a salesperson is to recognize that the cold call, even if welcomed, is still an interruption and proper etiquette requires respecting the limited time your buyer has available. In other words, the wise thing to do on a cold call is to finish before the buyer expects you to as a means to be welcomed back in the future.

The Appointment as a KPI

The more significant benefits of scheduled appointments are the numerous results created, thus making the scheduled appointment an important KPI as an effective as predictor of *future* success. Figure 9.2 illustrates the many predictable outcomes a salesperson can expect by planning meetings with buyers. An appointment, by definition, means the buyer will allocate the time to meet and even prepare questions for the meeting. Buyers commonly reveal unexpected business opportunities the salesperson had not considered, another benefit of a scheduled meeting. An appointment provides the allocation of time that can never be expected from a cold call.

The Appointment as a Key PERFORMANCE Indicator

Figure 9.2: An appointment is an unusual performance skill that doubles as both a KRI and KPI. As a key performance indicator, the appointment *"predicts"* better meetings will occur due to the expressed interest necessary from a potential buyer to schedule the meeting. This interests leads to the conclusions that time will be used efficiently; a prospect will reserve time for the meeting; a purpose and outcomes are established; and ultimately that the salesperson will enhance his or her professionalism and credibility.

The defined purpose of the appointment means that an anticipated outcome can be expected. The outcome is often a plan for a next appointment that can potentially be scheduled on the spot. The planning of a quality dialogue to take place during an appointment is a powerful demonstration of the seller's professionalism and credibility. In short, the appointment is a powerful predictor of future success.

The appointment is a definitive example of behavioral sales economics at work. It is a powerful predictor (KPI) of future outcomes that can be tested and proven through "trial and observation." Unlike most other skills in the profession, the appointment and the skill of calendar management prove to be the best illustrators (KRI) of sales competence at work. This singular, measurable activity can be included among many that will enable salespeople to establish the key performance indicators to improve sales process performance—microsales economics—and long-term sales success—macrosales economics.

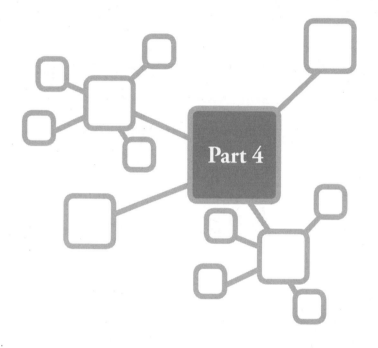

Part 4

MICROSALES
ECONOMICS

10

Introduction to Microsales Economics

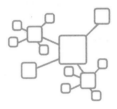

Sometimes Acronyms Help

Nobody likes to read books with acronyms or Russian names. These books force you to constantly page back and forth to clarify terminology and whether it was Vasily Razumikhin or Rodion Romanovitch Raskolnikov who committed the murder six chapters earlier. It's tedious. In this case, is was Raskonikov in *Crime and Punishment*, and I decided to use acronyms because they feel easier to read. I found myself concentrating too deeply on the words *microsales* and *macrosales* and was occasionally confused when reading them. It's easier to see the lowercase "i" or "a" as the subject reference in acronyms. Plus, truth be told, my fingers got tired of typing so many letters!

Statistical sales economics will be broken down into the categories of small-scale microsales economics (MiSE) and the larger picture of selling revealed by macrosales economics (MaSE) analysis.

Macrosales economics (MaSE with a lower case "a"), which will be covered later in the book, is about the big-picture study of sales performance and reveals answers about long-term sales goals and managing a sales campaign. Microsales economics (MiSE with a lower case "i") strives to answer questions about small-scale measurements of the sales process, transactions, and one-on-one business relationships.

Introduction to MiSE

Behavioral sales economics provided the analysis to improve individual behaviors. These behaviors are used in sets to build better relationships, host better meetings, and evaluate the quality of sales interactions. Traditional selling theory includes estimations about the effectiveness for the sales processes of prospecting, presentation, listening, and more. Behavioral sales economics eliminates guesswork by providing a model of trial, observation, and proactive consciousness. MiSE introduces KRIs and KPIs to measure the quality of interactions and relationships. In short, MiSE is the summation of the skills measured by behavioral sales economics.

MiSE provides numerous KPIs that enable a salesperson to measure the quality of sales calls; depth of business relationships; the valuation of a lead before pricing occurs; and, most importantly, how to create even more objectivity out of seemingly subjective performances. In turn, MaSE employs MiSE data to produce better long-term results. The benefit for salespeople is the surprising exposure of formerly invisible performance benchmarks.

The Invisible Salesperson

Selling is a unique profession because the performer operates unseen by managers and teammates. Unlike most other professions in which fellow employees occupy shared space where performance is easily observed, modeled, and evaluated by managers and coworkers, salespeople are habitually out of the office. They work independently and the most frequent observer of their performance is the buyer.

It's hardly in the buyer's best interest to teach salespeople how to sell better or negotiate more effectively. The salesperson is therefore left guessing, having no performance metrics to judge the quality of a sales call. The only person who can actually see the salesperson's performance with regularity, other than the buyer and anecdotal observations of a coworker or manager, is the salesperson.

The bigger problem is that other salespeople are also invisible to that salesperson and therefore there is no behavioral model to emulate. As pointed out several times, performance quality is not judged on performance actuality, but instead evaluated based on the single KRI of "success or failure." If a sale is made, performance competence is presumed. If not, the salesperson is considered incompetent.

Sales outcomes are hardly a suitable measure of performance because, as we know, success is often achieved by accident. Diet and KPIs come *before* weight loss and KRIs. It's not enough to simply measure your weight on the scale. The weight is the KRI of performance success; you have to put in the work and manage the KPIs. It is hard to argue with this logic and, moreover, almost impossible to believe that someone can lose a significant amount of weight and keep it off without a performance plan.

Interestingly, the same is *not* true for salespeople. They can be successful without putting in the right work or measurement of KPIs. The goal of MiSE is to identify performance benchmarks as objectively as possible to enable a salesperson to keep an honest and accurate measurement of performance. Otherwise sales success is accidental, which *occurs when no objective KPIs are established or measured as a link to predictable future KRIs.*

It happens and leads to the circular conversation of blame.

The Circular Conversation of Blame

When results are the only measure of performance competence, default interactions between a manager and salesperson devolve into circular conversations of blame. This concept is illustrated in the dialogue between our allegorical management hero, Abe, and his young sales pupil, Noah.

"How did the sales call go?" Abe asked.

Noah says, "Great. They liked what I offered."

Abe presumes Noah got the sale and enthusiastically asks, "So you got it?"

Noah, not having expected a sale in the first place wonders, "What?"

"The sale. That's the purpose, isn't it?" Abe asks, likely figuring he is doing his job by applying a little pressure to the performer.

"It is the purpose, yes, but the timing wasn't right," explains Noah. "The meeting was good, but I didn't get a sale yet."

"So...no. No sale?" Abe asks unemotionally. It turns out he isn't trying to judge or criticize, but merely understand, although Noah isn't feeling any relief.

"No, but it was a good meeting," Noah says reassuringly.

Abe asks with mounting interest, "Great! How do you know?"

"Not sure. I just have a good feeling."

It's an interesting statement for Abe to ponder. He has to wonder how a "good feeling" could be used as an objective results indicator and finally concludes aloud, "That's good I guess, although it seems the only way to know if you had a good meeting is when you actually get the sale."

Noah is left pondering before finally agreeing that a "feeling" might not be a good predictor of outcomes. It's hard to argue with Abe's statement and leads Noah to ask for help. "I'm open to ideas," he says. "Tell me how to gauge a sales call."

Our hero, Abe, has arrived at a critical moment of leadership. He can simply say to Noah, "You're the salesperson and I expect you to know how to make the sale happen." This is a statement that, of course, leads to the circular conversation of blame.

Noah would reactively reply, "I guess. But I'm asking for help. It feels like the manager should be able to give an answer."

Abe could say, "Nice try, but we pay you for the results."

Except...Abe does not say that. He is curious, always seeking truth, and wants to discover more. He wants to take the invisible performance and make it as visible as possible to himself and, more importantly, Noah.

Ask yourself how many times you finished a meeting with a good feeling, or even a bad one. You likely spent little time evaluating the reasons for your feelings and instead went along your way without self-reflection. Abe thinks more deeply.

The Time Value of Sales Activity

Abe pauses and finally admits to himself that Noah's challenge is fair. If Abe can't provide advice to improve the quality of a sales call or measure it, there is no justice in expecting his employee to do so. Abe ponders the idea of objective sales call measurement and can think of no other method than evaluating results, the KRI of successfully writing an order or not. He surprises Noah by readily admitting he isn't sure himself how to know if a sales call is productive or not.

This unsatisfactory answer makes both Abe and Noah uncomfortable. There must be some form of measurement that establishes the value of a sales call even when no actual transaction occurs. Together they brainstorm. They discover that each call can be measured by the total value of a transaction divided by the number of sales calls to create it. This turns out to be very appropriate measurement of time usage.

It's easy to realize that a $10,000 sale made in a single meeting establishes a $10,000 value for the interaction, but still leaves open the question about a meeting resulting in *no* transaction. Suddenly Abe suggests that a meeting resulting in no transaction can be valued later, after the sale is made. Thus, a sale that requires three meetings for the total value of a $10,000 transaction provides the answer. Each interaction is valued at $3,333, one-third of the total sale. This is a start, but with one problem.

A lot of sales calls, whether they are scheduled appointments or cold calls, result in no sale ever, particularly cold calls to prospects that often lead to dead ends. Abe considers this and sees no value in punishing a salesperson who is prospecting assertively by making cold calls. After all, it is a vital aspect of performance that can't be entirely worthless. Noah claimed he had a good meeting and Abe, an experienced salesperson, knows the feeling because he has had that experience even if he never stopped to logically evaluate his justification. If no sale is made, there has to be some value ascribed to that time.

He realizes the measurement of performance of a single sales call is challenging because there is no scale to "weigh" the result. In other words, even if he had the KPIs of performance, he wouldn't know how to value the quality of a single call in terms of outcomes, particularly when he considers that many lead to no sale. Unlike the dieter who steps on the scale and quickly ascertains the KRI of weight as the means to gauge the quality of dietary KPIs, there is no KRI available for Abe to measure for the short-term outcome of a sales call. Abe starts to wonder if the "weight" of the sales call could be woven into the equation. He figures that Noah, from coaching observations made in the field, is making about ten stops per week. Suddenly the math becomes clear in his mind! He scribbles some numbers on a piece of paper and comes to an important conclusion.

He figures that one (1) of those stops results in a $10,000 sale; three (3) stops to a single client result in another $10,000; six (6) more stops result in no sale...ever. The sales calls to prospects that never result in transactions are a bust by the standards of KRI measurement. In MiSE measurement, however, there is a value to calculate. Abe determines that the *average* value of each meeting is $2,000. He turns his paper to Noah, who studies the math. It is inescapably truthful and equips both of them with facts they can work with.

The Value of Sales Calls

	Number of Meetings	Sales Result (KRI)	Value Per Call (KRI)
	1	$ 10,000	$ 10,000
	3	10,000	3,333
	6	0	0
Totals	10	$ 20,000	$ 2,000

Figure 10.1: Each individual sales call produces different results. Taken individually, each sales call would be evaluated as either "success'" or "failure." A single meeting that results in a $1,000 sale is worth $10,000. If it takes three meetings to achieve a $10,000 sale, each meeting is worth $3,333. Sales resulting in no outcomes could be viewed as worthless, but are nevertheless required for overall job performance. Taken as a whole, ten (10) meetings are worth $20,000 or, *on average*, $2,000!

As illustrated in Figure 10.1, the value of each sales call for Noah's week equals, on average, $2,000. It's an important number. In any competitive endeavor, including the sales battle for market share, success is in the averages. The weekly totals for Noah provide that average. No chess move is guaranteed to work because the opponent is countering. It has been famously noted that Hall of Fame baseball players fail 70% of the time. Surely a superstar salesperson must expect failure. Success is only a percentage of effort.

This line of thought calls into question levels of practicality. Is it possible for a salesperson to get to this level of tracking and observation? The answer is, yes, it could be! A truly diligent salesperson could decide to count the number of face-to-face interactions with clients and prospects over the course of a week, month, and year. It's a pretty simple measurement that would reveal the average value of a sales meeting for an individual salesperson over a designated time frame. In fact, it seems like it might be one of the simplest measurements for the value of sales time.

The most successful business professionals establish the value of their time by the hour. One lawyer charges $200 per hour while another charges $2,000. One hair stylist charges $12.50 for a haircut while another charges $125. One keynote speaker charges $1,500 per speech while another charges $15,000. The huge difference between those little commas and the decimal points are the difference between mediocrity and excellence in time management valuation.

Working Smarter and Harder

Equipped with a formula for the time value of sales, the salesperson has the KRI to determine how well each sales call is going, revealing an opportunity to increase productivity by increasing the value of a sales call.

Abe asks Noah, "What do you see from the numbers?"

Noah appropriately responds, "It's great! I never thought about it like this, but I still don't see the answer to improve the result."

Abe knowingly points out, "There are two ways you can improve your performance. What are they?"

Noah pauses and suggests, "I guess I could make *more* calls. Or I could make *better* calls."

"That's it!" says Abe. "You could do one or the other…or both!"

Noah looks at his mentor and waits for further words of wisdom, which Abe delivers. "It would be foolish just to start making more random calls and presume your sales will improve. Making a lot of bad calls won't guarantee you $2,000 on every call. If you made ten more wasted calls last week, instead of doubling your sales by doubling your calls, you would have averaged only $1,000 per sales call. Successful improvement has to be both. Better *and* more calls."

Noah says, "Got it. Yes. I guess you do have to work smarter, *and* harder."

Abe quickly replies, "Agreed. Check this out!"

Abe uses the mathematics that establish a constructive and objective KRI for the *value of sales calls.* The analysis requires the count for a *total number of sales calls* to create a valid KRI for *the value of a single sales call.*

The Value of Sales Calls

$$\text{Sales Call Value (TF)} \quad = \quad \frac{\$ \text{ Sales Volume (TF)}}{\# \text{ Sales Calls (TF)}}$$

Figure 10.2: The value of a sales call can be established by time frame (TF). The *sales call value* is equal to the total sales volume dollars (or could be profit dollars) over a *time frame* divided by the number of sales calls in that same *time frame.* So the value of a sales interaction can be measured weekly, monthly, or even annually.

The formula includes the KPI for the number of sales calls over a time frame, which could be a week, month, or year. The KRI for the value of the call then becomes a simple matter of mathematics. Abe starts drawing and comes up with a formula that provides mathematical certainty about the *average value of a sales call*. His equation in Figure 10.2 illustrates that the sales volume is an easy result (KRI) to measure by simply looking at long-term sales data. Divide the sales volume over the time frame by the number of sales calls and you have your KRI, the monetary value of a sales call. Voila!

The Annual Value of a Sales Call

$$\$1{,}000 \text{ (Annual)} = \frac{\$500{,}000 \text{ (Annual)}}{500 \text{ Sales Calls (Annual)}}$$

Figure 10.3: The value of a sales call can be established by time frame (TF). The *sales call value* is equal to the total sales volume dollars (or could be profit dollars) *over a time frame* divided by the number of sales calls in that same *time frame*. So the value of a sales interaction can be measured weekly, monthly, or even annually.

Abe had established already that Noah was worth an average of $2,000 (one week) on ten sales calls during a week that netted $20,000 in total sales. If further investigation showed that Noah averaged ten calls per week in a territory generating $500,000 in annual revenue, his *sales call value* (Annual) would equal $1,000. Ten calls per week over a year that includes a two-week vacation equals the KPI of 500 sales calls. Annual sales of $500,000 divided by 500 sales call equals $1,000.

These data provide tools the salesperson can work with. Depending on geography, industry, sales cycle, and other factors, Noah might be able to increase the value of his total sales by increasing the number of sales calls, presuming they would be equal (or better) interactions. He can ensure the quality of his value per sales call by scheduled appointments, a vital KPI of future outcomes, rather than simply showing up for additional cold calls. In other words, an increase in scheduled appointments to new prospects would be a stronger predictor of future success than a bunch of random cold calls made while driving aimlessly in a sales territory.

Noah looks at Abe and points out that a salesperson could easily measure the number of sales calls by keeping a piece of paper in his visor. Abe nods and reminds him that he could use his calendar on the company software, but either way works. The more they discuss the concept, the greater their recognition of its value.

Abe says, "You know something, we could watch the monthly averages, too. We could measure how much your average sales call is worth."

Noah replies, "It would very cool to see if that number goes up as I get better at sales."

Abe replies, "Or goes down."

Noah hopes that doesn't happen and is surprised by Abe's quick response. "It could be natural," Abe says. "Which would you rather do? Make ten calls in twenty hours that results in ten thousand dollars or twenty calls in twenty hours that results in fifteen thousand dollars?"

Noah does the quick math and sees that the twenty hours that produces 50% more sales is better even if it means twice as many calls, particularly if the different number of sales calls can be accomplished in the same time frame of twenty hours. In the last example, the ten calls are worth $1,000 each, but only $500 per hour; the twenty calls are worth $750 each and also $750 per hour. Abe points this out and mentions it is an example of working smarter. He finally asks, "Of the two examples, which do you think will build more future business?"

Noah says, "Obviously the one with twenty calls in twenty hours. Eventually that fifteen thousand dollars will grow and my value per call, even if it drops in the short turn will eventually rise...*if* I keep doing the right things. I could even start tracking the value of both my hourly time and value per call."

Abe preempts that by saying, "Anyone willing to go to that extent of measurement would certainly be someone I'd admire, but I doubt I'd do it. It's a lot of work, but if you do it, let me know! I'd just track the calls and let my instinct about time take over. It's a pretty good start to measuring the value of sales conversations, isn't it?"

Noah eagerly agrees.

The two of them don't even realize it, but they have discovered the foundation for microsales economics (MiSE).

11

The Art of Measurement

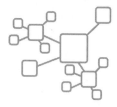

The Objectivity of Subjectivity

And the Academy Award goes to…the actor that a bunch of fellow actors rated #1 in the category by a consensus of their opinions. That's how measurement works in the arts and some athletic endeavors. Experts know the difference between excellence and mediocrity, even if it is a matter of opinion. The average person sees an actor playing the role of a woman experiencing grief. The expert sees a performer who simultaneously juts her head forward while sagging her shoulders as tears well up in eyes beneath furrowed brows. The poignant moment can be taken for granted by the audience in the context of a dramatic scene, but the pros see precision skill of several nuanced gestures and recognize greatness in the performance.

The ice skater finishes her routine and the primary performance criterion for the average observer is whether or not she fell while landing her spin. All other unadulterated Olympic skating performances look similar and beautiful to the average fan. The professional judges see differently. They know if the skater completed the correct number of rotations on each axel and toe loop. They can spot the accurate leg angle on a spin, proper edging techniques, and whether the skater correctly stuck each landing.

The art of measurement is a funny thing. Subjectivity to the amateur is a matter of objectivity to the expert. The art historian quickly noticed the inauthenticity that forensic analysis missed of the expensive statue purchased by the Getty Museum. The expert immediately recognized the size was wrong, proportions were off, and leg positioning was not in context of the period. *It takes an expert with experience to develop the subjective observations that become the objective evaluations of quality performance.*

It's true in the sales profession.

Easy Come Easy Go

What if Noah had made the sale and appeased Abe's initial objectives? What if the sale had occurred on the very first conversation between Noah and the buyer? The sale would have appeased the short-term needs of the Noah and Abe, yet failed to deliver the long-term results they seek. Most veteran salespeople agree that, in situations where long-term buying relationships must be established, a buyer who comes on board too easily is a cautionary indicator, a perfect example of the objective assessment of a subjective performance.

There is no math to prove it, but plenty of experience. A quick and easy sale in business-to-business relationships has shown many times to be a sale lost as easily as it was found. It suggests the buyer comes with financial baggage such a bad credit or high service costs. The easy sale often signifies that money was left on the table. The warning signs suggest there is value in a long selling cycle and begs the question: *If the sales cycle is expectedly long, how would a salesperson measure the value of performance in between the start of the dialogue and the close of the sale?*

Abe used historic data of sales volume and activity to establish Noah's value of sales interactions at $2,000 for a week and $1,000 per interaction on an annualized basis. These values are objective and easy to calculate if the performer is willing, like the honest golfer, to keep score. The problem for Abe is that the measurement is not a *performance* evaluation.

Abe ultimately concludes that the value of the sales call is a lagging indicator and therefore a value Noah cannot impact unless he makes behavioral changes. It's a valuable KRI, but leaves unidentified which *KPIs* to measure, what *actions* to repeat, and the *strategies* that increase the percentages of success. The salesperson needs to know what aspects of performance are the likeliest to elevate the final score. The salesperson needs to measure performance objectively *before the results are in*, a lesson I learned as a young car salesman.

The Objective Observation of Performance

It was a brief two-month tenure as a car salesman that was unenjoyable, albeit not without some powerful early lessons in selling. One lesson arrived the day I fielded an inbound phone call that was easy to interpret as a great opportunity. The buyer on the other end of the line was a hot lead who wanted a price on a car from our inventory. I believed an easy sale was in the making if the price were right and, therefore, promised to quickly return the prospect's call with a price after finding a car of his specifications.

Moments later I was sitting in my sales manager's office waiting for the pricing approval that never came. He told me, "People don't buy cars over the phone. Forget that lead and move on to a better one." I knew I had to call the buyer back and asked my manager what I was supposed to say if I couldn't provide a price. The manager said to be nice, but kindly request he come to the dealership if he wanted a price. I wasn't comfortable with the advice, but devised a plan to finesse the conversation with the buyer. I believed I could make the sale if only my manager would let me provide a competitive price.

Years later I can see my manager was practicing a form of consumer bid avoidance. To me, the phone call was objectively worth a potential sale of $15,000 for a brand new Oldsmobile. To the manager, the value of the lead was literally $0, unworthy of my time or his. I learned he was right when I called the buyer and told him we had the exact car he wanted and he could come in for a price and test drive. The buyer hung up so fast his phone left skid marks on my ear.

Conversely, I discovered the value of a real lead when a middle-aged man with unkempt hair and dirty clothing strolled into the same car dealership with his family. They looked poor and the situation was easy to judge. The man couldn't afford a car. He and his family were window-shopping to pass time on a Saturday afternoon. I stood nearby while waiting quietly for them to finish shopping and leave.

As they patiently strolled around, a veteran salesman pulled me aside and said, "That family is not here shopping. Dad wants to buy a car...*today!*" The sales veteran saw it as a hot lead and helped me engage. The signals that escaped my untrained eyes were easily picked up by the vision of trained ones. The veteran saw a $15,000 lead where I saw $0 and we soon sold Dad and the family a brand-new Oldsmobile!

In retrospect, the signals should have been pretty easy to see. The phone buyer made no physical commitment to the dialogue. I didn't recognize that a person in the pre-internet world would be highly unlikely to buy a car without seeing and driving it first. Besides, the buyer couldn't sign the papers and pay for it unless he were present. In short, the phone shopper was a very low percentage opportunity; the other one was high.

The available clues were identical for the other salesman, the manager, and me. However, in each situation, they objectively valued the leads with a level of experience I had not yet cultivated. Their perspectives were based on the wisdom that can only be accumulated by many years of subjective observation or by the conscious study of sales economics. The lesson provides insights for objective measurement of the seemingly subjective sales performance—i.e., behavioral sales economics. Just like an actor can evaluate the many choices of action on stage, so too can the salesperson evaluate the performance choices in a sales call.

In one performance I was tempted to price a car blindly to a stranger over the phone. Any credible expert would realize that would have been a waste of time. Had I given the stranger a price, I might still be wondering today if I had been bluffed by a competing car dealer. In the other situation I was literally waiting for an interested buyer to walk away. Had I simply waited for the family to leave, they would have purchased a car at another dealership. Fortunately, I was coached to avoid those inferior performance choices.

I learned the power of slowing down the process in the former situation and, in the latter, the lesson to not judge the value of a walk-in prospect. Just like the veteran actor sees performance choices and knows the difference, two veteran sales mentors interceded to help me objectively make better performance decisions during sales calls.

Developing Subjective Expertise

There is a marvelous story in *Blink* by Malcolm Gladwell during which a firefighting squad leader gets a sixth sense. He knew something felt wrong while fighting a fire and suddenly shouted at his crew. He commanded them to evacuate the building and, moments later, the floor that had been beneath them collapsed. During the interview afterward, he is asked what triggered his decision and could only say "a feeling."

After being pressed for details the squad leader replayed the scene in his mind. He recalled that the floor and room seemed hotter than usual. In their effort to put out the fire, adrenalin kicked in and most didn't notice the unusual level of heat buildup the squad leader sensed, nor the fact that the smoke was much greater and out of proportion to the size of the flames. It also wasn't responding to the amount of water relative to the size of the fire. Something was wrong and it was more than a feeling. It was years of experience that saved the lives of his firefighters.

The car sales manager, after years in the business, had experienced the phone call buying tactic on more than one occasion and knew the warning signals of a bad opportunity. His experience told him the request was probably not an indicator of sincere buying interest. The buyer might have been asking for a price to keep another car dealer honest. It might have been a bored salesman from a competing dealership playing phone games to get his jollies. Or perhaps the salesman was secretly conducting reconnaissance.

The buying signals were not right to the manager. The situation, in retrospect, was so obvious that it is astounding any salesperson would fall for it, yet it happened. To me. My inexperience, youth, and desire for a sale blinded me to the objective evaluation of subjectivity, specifically that a trained eye could see the lead as counterfeit.

In the construction products business, professional purchasing agents use this buying tactic every day, although they view it as efficient business communication rather than the counterfeit inquiry of the phone car shopper. The practice is institutionalized to the point that general contractors hire professional estimators to sit in offices, e-mail requests for bids to a network of suppliers, and categorize the pricing by products as the preparation for decision-making. No dialogue. No meeting. No desire for a business relationship other than the single transaction of supplying a single building with materials.

Besides being a sales role of low transactional dependability, the commercial construction sales position is highly impersonal. Salespeople in commercial construction have become so inured to the practice they assert there is no choice but to comply with so-called industry standards.

My experience, on the other hand, and that of many other industry veterans, is at a level of the sales manager who once mentored me during my brief stint selling cars. I have met salespeople who sell commercial construction products and manage to navigate through the impersonal hierarchy of the price acquisition committee to form powerful relationships with important influencers in the decision-making process.

The difference is the objective recognition of subjective situations. The request for a fast price quote that I once saw as an opportunity now gives me a bad "feeling" and knowledge that I must engage the bid avoidance presentation. I recognize that time can be used more productively elsewhere as a sort of opportunity cost time management system.

Opportunity cost, a classic term in traditional microeconomics, is defined as *the difference between the return on value of allocated resources to a purpose minus the return on value from alternative employment of those resources.* In this case, the resource is time. The practice of submitting blind bids to buyers unwilling to meet is something I shunned many years ago. I had developed the objectivity to recognize the action was like trying to close a million-dollar sale at a drive-through window. It just won't happen and, considering the opportunity cost of time, I quickly concluded that the two-hour preparation of a blind bid might be better spent prospecting elsewhere for a few higher percentage opportunities.

The power in the bid avoidance tactic is its ability to quickly flesh out the quality of a lead. A sincere buyer is willing to meet, discuss a problem situation, offer insights into buying criteria, and ask questions about the supplier's capabilities. It's easy for a salesperson to *know* about a sales opportunity and regard it subjectively as a lead; it's another thing entirely to secure time for a dialogue with a potential buyer and recognize the objective quality of a legitimate opportunity. In other words, the construction products salesman can't really rate a lead as legitimate just because a public report reveals a few homes are being built; there must be some sincere interest expressed from the builder.

One prospective buyer insists that you invest three hours creating a bid before an introductory meeting. You have no knowledge of the company goals, decision-making structure, or current buying habits. It is not a sincere level of interest. A second buyer suggests you set a time to discuss and understand her business challenges, meet team members, and assess ways your products might fit. Which of those leads would you rather have? Silly question, because the answer seems so obvious. Yet thousands of salespeople each day reactively pursue sales with the first buyer instead of proactively searching for the second!

Proactive Consciousness...Again

Abe established a measurement for the value of a sales call, even when no sale is made. He knew the *what*, but not the *how*. He and Noah had established the value of a sales call as a KRI while Abe wondered what activities would improve the KPI of each sales call. Abe's singular intent, as he starts to ask questions, is to discover the objectivity of performance and experience. He wants to know if there is something deeper to learn about sales behaviors and causality. He wants to know how to control the evolution of the sales process. He is seeking to discover and measure the art of sales *performance* measurement of a single sales call.

"Noah," Abe asks looking up thoughtfully, "You were onto something. You said it 'felt' like a good meeting. What did you mean by that?" Abe's questioning is not unlike the interview with the fire squad leader. Abe recognizes the feelings are not based solely on ESP or some mystical power; there is evidence to reveal.

Noah had worked for other managers only to discover they wielded authority, pressure, and reporting methods like weapons of control over performers. He was reticent to trust and was intentionally vague. "I'd say I had a sense, that's all. I probably shouldn't have said it. Maybe I was imagining things."

Noah knew, however, he was not imagining things and that the meeting was highly productive. He knew, but wasn't aware or confident enough to elaborate. Abe remained inquisitive. "Try," Abe says with rising passion, hoping to inspire the answer that Abe thought he already knew. "What gave you the feeling?"

Noah ponders and realizes his boss isn't about to give up. He scours his mind for a reason to justify his feelings and finally asserts, without realizing he sounds defensive, "He asked me to schedule an appointment for next week. So that seems like a good sign. I'm not trying to promise a sale or anything. But maybe that's why I had a good feeling."

"Yes," Abe says with beaming eyes. "Yes! That's it."

Noah is struck by the sincerity in Abe's tone and, when asked to share more, Noah mentions that the meeting was supposed to last only a few minutes, but fifteen minutes after it started, "my client asked his project manager into the office. We met and he had a lot of questions for me."

Abe nods knowingly as he starts adding up the factors that

might lead to success. He asks what Noah had learned about the potential new client. He wonders about the specifics of the company business and the dialogue that was shared. Noah lets down his guard, replays the sales call in detail in his mind, and then shares key points with Abe.

At the conclusion of their conversation, they agree that meeting the project manager was a telltale sign. The meeting lasted longer than planned. Noah reminded Abe that the meeting was a scheduled appointment instead of a cold call, an indicator that something was up even before the interaction took place. Those were some of the signs that led to a "feeling" for Noah. In fact, the success was more than a feeling; the success was evidenced by tangible, objectively measurable events.

This is how the KPIs of MiSE are developed. For most veteran salespeople, a time arrives when experience gives way to instinct. The veteran achieving desired results might assert, "I can't tell you how I do it; I only know that it's been working for years." This might be a great confidence boost for the claimant or perhaps a deflection of uncertainty from a performer who really doesn't know how success happened. In either case, the exercise in *proactive consciousness* is pivotal.

Imagine what would happen to the fire squad leader if he didn't take time to assess the situation *after* having made the right decision. It was later discovered that the fire had started in the basement of the building, a unique situation the squad leader may have not recognized at the time, but one that could be then "stored" as a potential situation for the future. Without proactive consciousness, he would have missed a vital moment of trial and observation that could produce better performance in the future. He also would have neglected a learning experience to pass on to other, younger performers so they could learn to properly assess unique fire situations in the future.

MiSE study reveals correlations between actions and results. This requires the manager and performer to bring unconscious performance of success to the surface level of proactive consciousness. It means the tactics that produce better results are evaluated objectively. It works in the science of selling and, in fact, *is* the science of selling. Abe used proactive consciousness to understand the details of Noah's meeting *after* it was complete as the means to measure and reshape future performance.

Abe tells Noah he has some ideas about calculating the value of a sales call.

"Haven't we already done that?" Noah asks while recalling the exercise of dividing sales over a time period by the number of sales calls.

Abe nods while squinting his eyes in thought. Noah recognizes new ideas are percolating in his mentor's head and waits for the inevitable comments of inspiration. "That's a result after the fact," Abe concludes. "We need to figure out how to actually calculate the performance quality of the sales call, not just the end result. We need a *predictive* number."

There next dialogue would reveal a clever method to establish more than a KRI for the value of a sales call by adding predictive KPIs!

"How can we do that?" Noah asks.

Abe lets Noah know, "You've already started."

12

Measuring the KPIs of a Sales Call

The Institutionalized Value of Performance

The scouts of major league baseball teams have been replaced, not with baseball experts, but with kids wielding computers. Stephanie Apstein reported in the May 6, 2019, issue of *Sports Illustrated* that veteran scouts have been left out wondering why their opinions have been replaced with computer prognostications. Apstein wrote that scouting meetings are "full of men in their 20s and 30s, speaking up from behind team-issued iPads or laptops, fluent in complex analytics."

One seventy-nine-year-old veteran scout lamented that, before he was fired, he was not even permitted to describe the baseball performances he saw in his "own words," but had to select them from predetermined descriptions of performance quality. In short, baseball has institutionalized the objective evaluation of subjective observations.

The writing wasn't exactly on the wall for old-school baseball scouts in 1985, but that was the start of the end. That was when Bill James revolutionized concepts in baseball statistics with his first book, *The Bill James Historical Baseball Abstract*, and coined the term "sabermetrics," a statistical process for analyzing the quality of baseball performers. Prior to James, baseball analytics were primitive and predictions about performance were highly subjective.

Statistics published for the average fan included just enough data to make the game interesting for spectators, but hardly helped managers and executives predict future outcomes. Then James analyzed what really mattered statistically in baseball. He concluded that the teams that outscore their opponents win games. Pretty simple…duh. It was obvious, but while traditional statistics adequately evaluate pitcher quality with the ERA, the average number of *earned runs allowed* in a game, there was no similar statistic for hitters.

James created a simple formula to analyze the quality of the player's offensive contributions and called it the "runs created" (RC) formula. His concepts were eventually applied by the early adopters who were prepared to revolutionize the process of management in the American game. Today virtually all teams employ complex statistical analyses to predict future outcomes.

James's work was popularized in Michael Lewis's book *Moneyball*, which later became a feature-length movie starring Brad Pitt as Billy Beane, general manager for the Oakland Athletics. Beane, a first-round pick by the New York Mets in 1980, never made it as a baseball player despite the "can't-miss" label applied to him as it has been to so many others in history. He missed, just like many other can't-miss prospects.

As a GM, he realized that a traditional approach to the game would not help his cash-strapped, small market team compete. So, he turned to sabermetrics to build a championship contender in spite of a payroll that was dwarfed by league powerhouses like the Yankees and Red Sox. Beane converted analysis of performance away from the opinions of scouts in favor of purely statistical scrutiny.

It is on this premise that microsales economics (MiSE) builds a thesis of sales performance. Instead of observing the looks, vocal patterns, embellished resumes, and vapid boasting of sales performers, MiSE enables a look at the statistics that will produce predictable, desired future outcomes.

Information Is the Game Changer

Imagine how prepared you would be as a hitter if you knew that your batting average doubled or tripled on balls in the lower half of the strike zone versus pitches over the waist. Your intention would shift completely to proactively seek pitches low in the strike zone. Consider that a team's winning percentage would rise significantly when it forced the opposing pitchers to throw more than one hundred pitches in a game. These statistics would change individual approaches to every at bat and team strategy.

This is one of the reasons baseball has changed significantly to the casual observer. Fifty years ago, games lasted two hours; today they last three or more. In 1968, ten starting pitchers completed more than sixteen games in a single season; four completed more than twenty. In 2018, fifty years later, not a single pitcher completed more than three.

The game has changed because pitchers are forced to throw more pitches. Relief pitchers come in as specialists to face only one hitter. Hitters are trained to be more selective. Managers have access to data that informs them about individual matchups and trends. A right-hand pitcher might hold opponents to a 20% chance of reaching base versus opposing right-hand hitters while allowing a whopping 35% of left-hand hitters to succeed. In a clutch situation, a manager must make the decision to pull his right-hand starter versus a left-hand hitter as the best percentage chance of success.

Of course, all this baseball talk has little to with the profession of selling, but everything to do with the power of data and knowledge. The work of thought leaders in the sport of baseball took the concept of KPIs and applied them to the predictable desired results (KRIs). The same can be accomplished in sales.

MiSE provides insights into sales performance that parallel the concepts in baseball sabermetrics. If a season of wins and losses is the goal, then each game matters. Outcomes are created by quality of one-time individual performances that, added up, produce the necessary wins for championship seasons. In the same way, long-term sales success begins with the analysis of individual sales interactions that, added up, provide the sum total of an annual performance, perhaps better thought of as a "full *sales* season."

Lao Tzu, the famous Chinese philosopher, was reputed to say, "The journey of a thousand miles begins with a single step." A baseball campaign of more than six thousand at bats begins with a single pitch. A sales campaign of a year begins with a single call. It is from this premise we launch our analysis to discover the KPIs of a single sales call.

The Quality of an At Bat

For decades, the evaluation of success for a player at the plate was measured by the results. Today, the analysis of performance is detailed to the degree that every player has a plan prior to stepping to the plate. Each player strives for a "quality at bat." On the chance that some readers are simply not baseball fans, it merits a quick definition of an "at bat." (For baseball fans, they will recognize that the statistics are really the measurement of a "trip to the plate," because a sacrifice or walk does not count as at bats, but that is grasping at straws to worry about the delineation.)

In baseball, there are nine innings during which each team gets to play on offense until they reach three outs. Each player on opposing nine-man squads takes turns trying to get on base and eventually score. Prior to Bill James and sabermetric analysis, the primary judgment of performance was a player's batting average, which tells only part of the story. It turns out that a player doesn't need to even hit the ball! He can just stand there while the pitcher eventually misses the target area four times, resulting in a "walk" for the hitter. Anyone who has played little league baseball or coached a team knows that a walk is as good as a hit.

The funny thing is that kids didn't believe it. They wanted to hit the ball because it was more fun and, more importantly, a walk doesn't increase your batting average. There is a separate statistic that combines hits *and* walks to produce an on-base percentage. So a player with a respectable 28% batting average would be a valuable asset on a team, but not if he never walks and therefore gets on base only 28% of the time, somewhere near the lower quarter percentile of major league averages.

A player with a 24% batting average who walks enough to get a 40% on-base percentage would be performing above the 95th percentile of performers in the league. Billy Beane concluded that you'd be much wiser to forego the glamor of a high average, expensive player when a less touted player with a superior on-base percentage is available.

Today, a quality at bat is measured (Figure 12.1) by accomplishing any one of the following performance benchmarks: a hard hit ball, an extra base hit, forcing the pitcher to throw six or more pitches, a sacrifice bunt or fly, and a walk. A player who smacks a ball that is caught for an out is credited with a quality at bat, even though he didn't achieve the desired result.

KPIs
- Hard Hit Ball (HHB)
- Extra Base Hit (XHB)
- 6+ Pitches
- Sacrifice Bunt (SAC)
- Sacrifice Fly (SF)
- Walk (BB)

Figure 12.1

If a fielder has to dive to catch a ball hurtling at eighty miles per hour five feet off the ground, it's a "hard hit ball." Consider that a squib off the end of the bat or a lucky pop just out of reach to the outfield is not considered a quality at bat even though the player gets on base. The reasoning is simply that accidents cannot be repeated. Even a strikeout is considered a better performance than an accidental hit if the batter manages to force the pitcher to throw more than six pitches. Good performance can be repeated and produces predictable results.

Success is, of course, not judged by a good try. The real purpose of the endeavor is predictable results and, ultimately, wins. In the case of baseball performance, Bill James proved it. Managers listened. Executives did too and changed their payroll philosophies and office structure. The methodology creates a set of KPIs and the foundational game plan for success that is not based on measuring only the runs created after the fact, but on the moment-by-moment in game performance.

Predictable KRIs

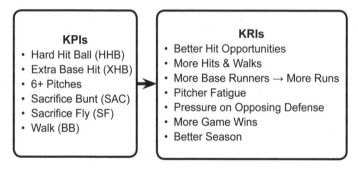

Figure 12.2

The predictable outcomes should come as no surprise. As you see in Figure 12.2, the correlation to KRIs is significant. As players on a team take more pitches and wait for ideal ball locations, hit opportunities improve. More hits are created and, if the batter is patient, more walks. More base runners, the simplest and most vital aspect of Bill James's work, equals more runs.

Bill James measured the importance of base runners and concluded that it is such a vital statistic that some teams and players should never try for a stolen base. The risk of the out, for players who get caught too frequently, does not offset the value in the improved positioning of the runner. Having runners on base matters.

More runners put pressure on defenses and exposes weakness. As pitchers are forced to throw more, exhaustion sets in and the chances for mistakes increase. All these little factors add up for a team that will send over 6,000 players to bat in a single season. A team that achieves significantly more quality at bats than its opponents will win more games and have a better season.

For this reason alone, the opinions of scouts matter less when not based on a consensus of objectivity. In short, the KPIs of a quality at bat in baseball have significant impact on results (KRIs) and, more importantly, provide an insight into MiSE that we can apply to individual sales calls.

Defining the KPIs of a Sales Call

Noah and Abe discovered and agreed that some indicators of progress included the fact that an appointment had been scheduled. Noah admitted that the purpose of the call was to learn about the customer's business. "I really didn't have a specific product to discuss or proposal to make," Noah admitted.

Abe said, "I don't think that matters. The fact that you had an introductory meeting and the client blocked out time says something, doesn't it?"

Noah agreed, "I sense they might be having problems with their current supplier, but it didn't come up…at least not yet."

"Doesn't matter," Abe said while considering the idea of a sales scorecard. "In fact, I think it might be better that it hasn't come up yet. Perhaps the buyer was vetting *you*. It sounds like you had a pretty good meeting based on the fact your prospect allocated time and even invited someone else in the meeting."

KPIs of the Sales Call

1 – Cold Call
2 – Warm Call
3 – Appointment
1 – New Contacts Engaged

Figure 12.3

Noah agreed and watched as Abe scribbled some notes on paper. "What's a KPI?" Noah asked. After hearing the explanation, he noticed the points Abe had ascribed to the appointment and the other KPIs. "I can see how you give three points for an appointment and only one for a cold call, but what's a warm call?"

Abe settled in to explain that a lot of sales interactions take place at flexible times, but are scheduled nevertheless. "For example, we often need to support our clients with a brief service call. As a window salesman, I frequently offered my business-to-business clients the service of keeping the screens in our warehouse until construction was complete, which I naturally charged for. By the time my client wanted them, we didn't always schedule firm appointments. I just got them there on the day they wanted. Make sense?"

Noah nodded, "I do that a lot, too. Sometimes I have to drop off samples. Or leave brochures. Things like that, but I don't have scheduled appointments."

"Do they know you're coming?" Abe asked.

"Sometimes," Noah admitted. "Not always."

Sales Call Scheduling Value

Cold Call – Unexpected Pop-In (or Phone Call) with a Prospect or Client

Warm Call – Scheduled Meeting at a Location with a Purpose within a Flexible Time Frame

Appointment – Scheduled Meeting (or Phone Call) with a Purpose, Location, Time, and Place

---

Figure 12.4

"If they know you're coming and plan to meet you, it's a warm call. It's a prearranged meeting with a purpose at a flexible time. If they don't know you're coming and you just hope to catch them at the right moment, that's a cold call."

"Aren't they the same?" Noah asked.

Abe said, "Not really. You're relying on luck with a cold call to catch someone at a place and time without their expectation. A warm call is a sort of 'appointment-lite' because the buyer knows there is a place you'll be meeting even if the time is flexible. The goal is an interaction they see as a value you provide. It's a fine line, but let's go with it for now. The key is that a cold call is still valuable, but not as valuable as someone expecting you at a place, and definitely not as valuable as a scheduled meeting at a defined time and place."

Noah agreed and asked if that means an appointment is worth six points because you add all three.

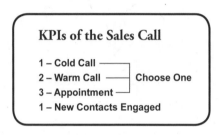

Figure 12.5

Abe chuckled and thought about it. "Let's just say to choose one," he concluded. "I have no idea why, but it's a start. I don't want to diminish a cold call so much and definitely a warm call is valuable, too. So let's just say to choose one. We'll add a point because you met someone new at the organization. That is always a powerful indicator, not only of interest, but a way to strengthen your relationship for the long term.

"So the meeting was a planned appointment established *before* you arrived. That's worth three points. What else made it a good sales call besides having an appointment and meeting the project manager?" Abe asked.

"Well," Noah pondered for a moment and finally said, "I thought I took good notes. I have the information about the company and their plans. I met the buyer and also the project manager and got their business cards. I put them in my CRM database. And I have notes on the product they want me to show them."

Abe was taking notes while listening and then looked up with surprise and a smile. "What do you mean *the product they want you to show them*?" He sat back waiting for Noah to explain.

"Well, like I said," Noah began with a near apologetic tone. "I didn't get any specifications for a project and wasn't asked to price anything. So I can't really call it a lead, but at least they are interest in seeing the product."

Abe looked directly into Noah's eyes to prepare him for the news. "That's a lead, Noah. It's the best kind!"

Noah warned that the buyer wasn't even interested in pricing yet.

Abe said, "Perfect! That's even better!" He was beaming as he always did when new sales ideas were flowing and positive events were blossoming. "If they had asked you to bid or price, it would have been worse. If you ask me, a dialogue about product applications, project goals, administrative issues, and delivery plans should come first. That should happen before a price. If you had told me they wanted a price, I would have still considered it a lead. The fact that they want to talk more before pricing means they are serious about a relationship. Do you see that?"

Noah thought about it. It surprised him to receive so much praise for a meeting that, to his thinking, resulted in no sale. The more he considered Abe's perspective, the more sense it made. He described the dialogue in more detail and explained, "It's funny. I could tell they really needed to discuss the product, but I didn't know why."

Abe said, "That's okay. If you can schedule a next meeting with them, you'll find out then."

Noah said, "It already is scheduled. We're meeting next Thursday at our office."

Abe set his pen down again and stared in amazement. "This is excellent," he said. "So the meeting was an appointment, worth three points just because it was scheduled before you arrived and, during the meeting, you scheduled a follow-up meeting. Those two aspects of performance are powerful indicators of interest! We'll give two points for the meeting you scheduled as a follow-up to the appointment. That's five points right there!

"I feel silly that I first asked you a few minutes ago about taking an order, which you didn't. Instead you described that it 'felt' like a good call." Abe used his fingers to depict quotation marks that, if anything, held his own comments in some form of mild mockery while he wordlessly was elevating Noah to a pedestal of esteem. "You have a meeting scheduled and they want to meet you again. Here on our turf! Fantastic! I suspect that getting them to our office is worthy of something, but that's not a feat you can accomplish every time. So we'll leave that off the scorecard for now and construct it this way."

Abe scribbled new criteria onto his KPI sales scorecard. Noah watched.

KPIs of the Sales Call

1 – Cold Call ⌐
2 – Warm Call ⊢ Choose One
3 – Appointment ⌐
2 – New Lead
1 – New Contacts Engaged
1 – Documentation
1 – Endorsed Follow-Up Plan
2 – Next Interaction Scheduled

Figure 12.6

Abe finished his scribbling and concluded that there were about ten points a salesperson could chalk up for a high-quality call. He had actually given only one point to the scheduling of the next meeting and decided it was too important before deciding to give it two.

"What's the difference between an 'endorsed follow-up plan' and a 'next interaction scheduled?'" Noah asked.

Abe said, "It's possible that a buyer will ask you to fulfill a task. It could be anything such as send a brochure, e-mail a credit app, mail a sample, or anything that is a task for you to fulfill even though you don't have the next meeting scheduled. It's a fine line and both are indicators, but having the next meeting is a very strong one. Do you agree?"

Noah thought about it and realized it gave him something he could work on objectively as a means to make all of his customer meetings better. "Yes, I like it," Noah said with rising enthusiasm.

"Noah," Abe said with finality. "I think we're onto something here. It seems like your feeling was more than correct. If anything it was an understatement. If you have sales calls like that with any degree of consistency, I think your career will soar."

Noah looked at the list and silently checked off every criterion in the box as Abe heaped praise on his student. "Your meeting was scheduled *before* you walked in as an appointment—three points. Plus you managed to schedule the *next* meeting while you were there—two more points! You met someone new—one point—and heard they have very legitimate interest in a specific product we sell and want the product specifications—two more points. You put the information into your CRM—one more point for documenting your activity. And you met the project manager, someone you didn't know before the appointment—one more point.

"That's ten points total," Abe said. "The points are obviously a subjective calculation, but they truly paint and objective picture of quality. Don't you agree?"

Noah looked at the scorecard and said, "I did have a good feeling. Now I can see why. It's like that proactive consciousness you talked about. I had to review afterwards what happened because I was too focused on my client in the meeting. This really makes sense." Then Noah looked up and asked, "Does it really count if I met the extra decision-maker by accident?"

Abe smile and said, "Of course! That being said, doesn't this prove that maybe you should do it intentionally the next time?"

"Definitely!" Noah said. "There is one thing, though. As I think about it, I've called this company before and couldn't get a meeting. So it's not exactly a 'new lead.'"

"Not true," Abe said with conviction. "In fact, had you

listed it as a lead before, I might have disagreed. If the company had said, 'You can give up some pricing, but we're not going to change unless you're way lower than your competitor,' I wouldn't have called this a lead. A *new lead* is a situation in which *the buyer expresses overt interest in a specific product or service you offer*. It's kind of a subjective thing, but I think you get it. Are they sincerely interested?"

"I think so," Noah said.

"I know so."

"How?" Noah asked.

"Think about it," Abe said. "What are the signals?"

Noah saw the answer right away. "I met someone new when the buyer brought in the project manager."

"And...?" Abe asked.

"Not sure," Noah said. "Isn't that enough?"

Abe chuckled and said, "Yes. It is enough. But we're not just doing this to evaluate this lead. We're working on a process of proactive consciousness. What if you hadn't met the project manager, but the client had still agreed to visit our office for the next meeting? What would that have told you?"

"It would have told me he was a serious buyer with interest," Noah responded while nodding knowingly. "I like this process," he concluded. "It's under my control. I don't know if it will lead to a result, but I like it. It gives me a scorecard to work with."

Abe assured him that there was no way of knowing it would lead to a result "in this case."

"What do you mean in this case?" Noah asked.

"Stuff happens," Abe said with a casual shrug. "You might not get this one. But...BUT...if you have enough meetings like this, I think the value of your sales calls will be a lot more than two hundred dollars per sales call. Remember? That's how we started this?"

"Riiiight," Noah said with a sigh while wheels were spinning in his head.

"We know how to value a call after the fact and, more importantly, we know how to raise the value of it," Abe said. "What do you think will happen if you have a lot more calls like today?"

The KRIs of the Sales Call

Noah and Abe looked at each other quietly and then started brainstorming at a frenetic pace. Abe could barely write fast enough to keep up.

"Better meetings with prepared clients that are expecting you," Abe said.

"I bet that some of them will come up with ideas to talk about I hadn't considered if they know I'm coming," Noah said.

"I agree! You'll be more prepared too because you'll be thinking about it, visit their website, and talk to other people about the company. You'll both be prepared," Abe concluded.

They both agreed that time would be used more efficiently and that more people would be known in an organization. "Ever lose a customer because your only contact left the company?" Abe asked.

"Yep," Noah admitted. "Hate to say it, but yes."

"Me, too," Abe admitted matter-of-factly. "Part of the learning process. What else will happen?" he asked to get back on task.

They both agreed that more sales opportunities and leads would be revealed. They agreed that the professionalism of having a planned meeting would differentiate them from their competitors. The lengthier dialogue would produce better margins and higher profitability. Noah finally concluded, "More points on the scorecard today will produced more results later. Lots more!"

Abe smiled as the two ran out of gas. The agreed there were probably flaws in their final list and the point system was rudimentary, but it was something. They stared at their diagram.

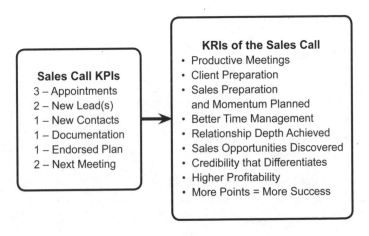

Sales Call KPIs
3 – Appointments
2 – New Lead(s)
1 – New Contacts
1 – Documentation
1 – Endorsed Plan
2 – Next Meeting

KRIs of the Sales Call
• Productive Meetings
• Client Preparation
• Sales Preparation and Momentum Planned
• Better Time Management
• Relationship Depth Achieved
• Sales Opportunities Discovered
• Credibility that Differentiates
• Higher Profitability
• More Points = More Success

Figure 12.7

The Sales Secret

In my previous book, *The Sales Secret*, Abe had shared the secret to closing more sales with other pupils and actually called it *"the next step."* He believed the closing process was the most mismanaged and poorly taught aspect of the profession. "The whole idea of asking for the order is overblown," he was fond of saying. "Managers pressure their salespeople to close deals without recognizing the reality of the situation."

The Sales Secret illustrates the microsales process in detail by defining a three-step sales call that begins by *planning* a purpose with a client or prospect prior to the sales call. The second step is the actual meeting, *during* which the salesperson employs all the skills of microsales—e.g., presentation, listening, handling objections, building rapport, prospecting, and closing. The third step occurs *after* the sale is complete when the salesperson documents important issues, follows up on commitments, and conducts a review that I have now defined as proactive consciousness.

In *The Sales Secret*, Abe explained how a fast sale is a warning sign. He explained, asserts actually, that the process should be slow if results are going to be lasting. Ultimately, Abe illustrates that the reason for the next meeting should be established during the existing one. The goal is to end a meeting with a purpose for the next meeting the buyer accepts and values. He called it "the next step" and considers it the sales secret to success.

Noah was experiencing all the same coaching as Abe's other pupils. Not surprisingly and like the others, Noah confessed, "I struggle figuring out that 'next step.' I feel pretty lucky that

I got the next meeting. To be truthful, it was the buyer's idea to schedule a visit to our office. I didn't suggest the idea. He did."

Abe explained. "It's the hardest thing in the sales profession. The art of closing, *and it is an art,*" he emphasized, "is a three-step process."

Noah nodded and pleased Abe by taking out a pen to write.

"Step one," Abe said. "Figure out a reason to help. It could be a product you offer. Or it might be a referral. Or it could be advice. Or anything. There are a ton of reasons. That's the art. At first, most salespeople are looking for sales opportunities. As the salesperson matures, other reasons for dialogues are discovered. You will learn how to leverage your knowledge. Got it?"

"Got it," said Noah.

Abe explained that the real art of selling is finding that reason. "It's the hardest thing to learn at first, but over time it will come easier. The more you know about a client, the more ways you can help. Step two! Ready?"

"Ready."

"Recommend the reason for a next meeting to your client. Literally say, 'We should get together to discuss X...or Y...or Q...or whatever idea you've come up with. Got it?"

"Got it."

"Step three," said Abe. "Get it on your calendars. Plural. Send an electronic invite. Watch the buyer put it down on their calendar if possible. If the buyer isn't committed to a date, time, and place with a specific purpose for meeting, it's not an appointment. Got it?"

"Got it," said Noah. "One more question?"

"Ask as many as you want."

"What are the things I need to know about my client to figure out these next steps?"

"Good question," said Abe with a smile. "In fact it is *the* question. Let's figure it out."

13

The Economics of Business Relationships

The KRI of the Relationship Sales Call

"I figured it out!" Noah said. "I can calculate how much I'm worth on every sales call with each customer using the math you did before."

"Excellent!" Abe said. "How so?"

"Well, I'm not sure how to clarify this, but it seems like I could use my time better by analyzing how I invest it with customers," Noah said. "So, I call on Allied Construction about twice per month, right?"

Abe was intrigued and loved how his pupil was thinking. "Go on," he said.

"You figured out my time is worth about $1,000 per sales call and I get $15,000 worth of business per year from Allied. So that time is worth $625 per sales call. That is $15,000 divided by twenty-four, which is two sales calls per month. So it seems I am losing $325 per call to them."

Abe sat and thought about Noah's numbers. It wasn't just the numbers that impressed him, but more that he had a student who was thinking proactively about the concepts and now adding to them! It was a moment when Abe said the dialogue starts to evolve from a mentor-pupil relationship toward peer-to-peer dialogue. "That's awesome!" he said. "What does it tell you?"

"That I should call on Allied less," Noah said.

"Or get more business from them," Abe said without confrontation, but as a form of brainstorming.

"Yes," Noah said beaming with pride because of the praise received from his mentor. "But it's a valuable thought, right?"

"It's awesome," Abe said. "Is it a KPI or a KRI?"

Noah pondered and finally concluded, "I think it's a KRI. It gives me data, but not the way to change it. I need to shift my performance to increase the value of my time, both with Allied and in general."

"I totally agree," Abe said. "You have to increase your influence."

Closing Ratios Rise with Authority

A physical therapy department inside hospital was staffed with frustrated practitioners. Their patients were being assigned exercises that they didn't complete. As the spouse of a physical therapist (PT), I know in great detail the level of expertise, schooling, and specialized practice it takes to become a quality PT. I also know that the real goal of physical therapy is to help the patient regain independence through improvement of motion. The patients, on the other hand, either believed the PTs should do all the work or, for some other reason, didn't take the exercise advice.

This was the challenge Robert Cialdini experienced and wrote about in *Influence: The Psychology of Persuasion*. In the case of the hospital department, he investigated why patients were ignoring the advice of PTs and discovered that it was a matter of *authority*. The patients recognized doctors by their well-established authority based on diplomas and earned credentials. His team learned in interviews that patients didn't recognize the credentials of the PTs until a suggestion was made. The PTs were advised to place their diplomas and professional certifications in prominent locations as the means to boost their authority. According to his October 2001 article in the *Harvard Business Review*, "The result was startling: Exercise compliance jumped 34% and has never dropped since."

I have already asserted that a challenge for salespeople is a lack of credentials. Cialdini's research determined that authority results when expertise is recognized, thus creating a problem for salespeople. In the absence of credentials, no third party is going to bestow authority on a salesperson. It must be earned.

The Fallacy of the Friendship Foundation

Business relationships are unique; they are bigger than friendships and come with different levels of responsibilities. A business relationship that is built on friendship is always at risk. I called it the "fallacy of the friendship foundation."

I had just delivered this message at a seminar when an attendee strolled toward me and said, "Let me give you a tip and it is A-OK if you share it with your audience." I waited for his advice and heard him say, "I believe the moment you can call your customer a 'friend,' you have succeeded." I thanked him for his insight while wondering why he would express a belief that contradicted the advice he heard me offer just moments earlier. I think he wanted to defend a career during which he regularly tried to become close friends with his clients, like many salespeople do, as the primary strategy for sales success.

The fallacy of the friendship foundation in business is that the obligations of a friendship are based on willingness while the business obligations include financial consideration. Friendships are low obligation relationships where the scorecard of reciprocity (another factor of influence revealed by Cialdini) is a low priority. The moment money changes hands, the relationship dynamic does, too. Business relationships are a quid pro quo exchange of money for services where reciprocity is demanded. Friends expect special pricing and favors above and beyond the price of the original transaction or, in other words, reciprocity *plus more*.

Randy, a home improvement contractor I was mentoring, received pressure from a neighborhood friend attempting to leverage the personal relationship by seeking a lower price on a kitchen-remodeling project. I advised Randy to hold firm on the price in anticipation of additional combative dialogues and requests for favors to come. Randy believed the friendship would facilitate a cooperative business relationship and decided to relent on the discount request.

I warned Randy that the future two-dollar beer his neighbor casually offers might evolve into a three hundred dollar service call performed for free on the basis of the entitlement his soon-to-be ex-friend feels due. Randy pondered that advice as I tacked on a second suggestion that he make sure to include a stipulation that requires the buyer to sign off on any changes to the original contract for additional products or labor that would occur during the construction process.

Randy did not hold his price. He did not include a clause for contract addendums. He did not create price stipulations for additional services provided after project completion. In the end, the buyer was slow to submit his final payment because of project changes he thought were verbally agreed upon. Later, Randy told me that he went to a cookout during which the neighbor asked Randy to perform a quick service adjustment to a faucet and door, neither of which he had installed! Randy said it was the last cookout he'd attend at his neighbor's house and, moreover, wished he had charged more for the sale or even passed on it.

The fallacy of the friendship foundation cuts both ways in that salespeople rather than customers come to expect special consideration beyond the defined scope of the business relationship. Early in my career I spent a lot of time socializing with clients while traveling a three-state territory. One day, Mark, the manager of a dealership in Charleston, West Virginia, let me know that the company was dropping my product line. I was shocked because, even though my company had 100% product defect and was verging on bankruptcy, Mark and I had developed, in my mind, such a good friendship. (The nerve of some people!) Mark assured me that I was always welcome to visit and golf with him again when in town.

I lost an account worth a half million dollars and, truth be told, didn't have the desire to golf with Mark again. The honest feedback I had to give myself is that my services were deficient. I took the relationship for granted. My employer had problems that I·didn't properly address with Mark. Those were the obvious flaws in my performance I could identify then. As an experienced veteran, I can now identify more. I deserved to lose the business. Mark found a better supplier who, even though not a friend, would provide more business benefit.

Friendship does not preclude successful business relationships, but is by no means a guarantee of them either. The relationship must be based on business benefit to the buyer while also creating profitability for the seller.

Behavioral sales economics lesson #1 about business relationships: *Friendship can be a byproduct of a solid business relationship, not the foundation of it.*

The Product Needs Fallacy

The salesperson who gets past the "fallacy of the friendship foundation" must also overcome the "product needs fallacy." The seller might be selling a product, but the buyer isn't buying one. The buyer is fulfilling a purpose. The buyer has a problem to solve, or a dream to pursue, or a necessity to fill.

Behavioral economics has proven that the motivations and decision-making process for buyers is contingent on diverse and unpredictable factors. Business entities rarely buy products for the sake of ownership, but instead to repurpose the product as a sales asset. Consumers buy products to satisfy economic needs, status, esoteric fulfillment, and other motivations. The successful salesperson first listens before promoting products and services. I learned this thirty years ago in a bookstore.

Swim with the Sharks Without Being Eaten Alive by Harvey Mackay was sitting on the shelf. The title was interesting so I scanned the book to find a list he called the "Mackay 66," sixty-six things you should know about your customers. It included the buyer's vacation habits, the spouse's interests, the kind of car(s) driven, and even favorite items on restaurant menus. I concluded the list contained ridiculous and useless information far beyond anything necessary to make a sale. Therefore the book should be purchased instantly!

Clearly this man was thinking very differently than I was. More importantly, Harvey Mackay built an envelope company, became a best-selling author, and is a hall of fame speaker in the National Speakers Association. The learning lesson to take from the Mackay 66 is that information you first gather about your customers has nothing to do with you and the products you sell; the information is about the client.

Behavioral sales economics lesson #2 about business relationships: *It's not about the product. The most important thing to understand is the client.*

The Fallacy of Open-Ended Questions

Sales 101 teaches the skill of asking open-ended questions. It's never been a lesson I favor, mostly because I think it's wrong. The skill of discovery comes in listening and doesn't stop there. It's not about listening randomly, but in knowing what information you need to glean whether by questions, observation, research, or any other means.

Open-ended questions that begin with the words who, *what, when, where, how,* and *why* theoretically force the responder to elaborate in ways that reveal key information. The problem is they don't necessarily work and, more importantly, are not always necessary. Open-ended questions are a subset of the listening process. If the salesperson can't identify the information to be heard, it won't matter what questions are asked. Conversely, if the salesperson can identify information without a question, then there is no need to ask it. Listen first.

Imagine the copier salesman who asks an office manager of a law firm, "What are your biggest problems with your document duplicating process today?" It's a wonderful and professional open-ended question. It is a great start to a dialogue and suddenly falls flat when the office manager responds, "Truthfully nothing. We love our copiers and the service. We plan to renew our lease in the coming weeks. Sorry, but we're happy." The great open-ended question got a much closed answer.

On the other side of town, a copier salesman asks a different office manager, "Is your copier working good?" Clearly this salesperson missed the sales training seminar on open-ended questions as well as the grammar session on adjectives versus adverbs. A manager would object to such a poorly constructed question, because the buyer can answer "yep" or "nope." In this case however, the answer is a tension release from the buyer of frustration and anger. She laments the problems the company has had from the poor quality of prints to constant service calls; from lack of response to color consistency issues; and missed client deadlines as a result of printing delays. At the conclusion of the buyer's diatribe, she says, "The day our lease is up next month, the copier company better be here to pick up their stuff because we're leaving it on the street!" The poorly constructed question by the second salesman got a very open answer.

Which prospect would you rather have, the satisfied prospect or the angry one in need of a new supplier? Silly question of course, but it proves a point. The key to listening is not crafting the right question, but in hearing the right information.

Behavioral sales economics lesson #3 about business relationships: *The quality of discovery is not in the questions, but resides in the answers.*

The Fallacy of Presumptive Fit

Salespeople are instructed *how* to make the sale and rarely taught to investigate *if* a sale should be made. Critical managers often pressure salespeople to know *why* they failed. It is rarely an acceptable answer for a salesperson to say the supplier wasn't a good fit for the buyer at this time. Sometimes the timing is off. Sometimes the other supplier is doing a great job. Sometimes the seller just doesn't have the right product. Sometimes the salesperson is just late. To assume there must be a reason to make *every* sale is the fallacy of the presumptive fit.

I spent many years as a commercial salesman for a window manufacturer where architectural specifications drove purchasing decisions. The process involves a long gestation period during which an owner selects an architect who provides a schematic rendering of the project style for approval. The next phase is design documentation where dimensions are finalized, budgets are considered, and products are selected. The last phase includes construction documentation where detailed drawings and specifications are written. Finally, project bids are requested.

This is the moment a desperate salesman, who hasn't been involved during any early stages of the process, discovers his product was not included as an approved or accepted brand. He contacts the architect with the hope that six to eighteen months of planning and dialogue can be scrapped for the convenience of a salesperson eager to make a sale. My counsel to salespeople in this situation is to contact the architect and reference the project while being prepared to hear the architect say, "I appreciate the call, but that project is let. We don't want to change a spec at this stage."

At that point, the salesperson should say, "I wouldn't suggest for a moment that you should change anything on this project. But if the work is indicative of your typical design and project scope, my company's products would be a very good fit on future projects. Can we set up a brief introductory dialogue?"

I call this aikido selling. Aikido is the martial art where you use your adversary's momentum to your advantage while trying to do your opponent no harm. This is one of those tactics you will need to test for yourself with trial and observation, but you will discover it is one of the most powerful assets in your sales arsenal.

Open any introduction to a prospect with the suggestion to determine if you are a "fit" and barriers to resistance will instantly be overcome. It's even better if, rather than using it as a clever tactic, you mean it! It is the openhearted way to establish meaningful client dialogues.

Behavioral sales economics lesson #4 about business relationships: *Do not presume you are a fit for the buyer until you know.*

Establishing Your Authority

In the United States and Canada, business dialogues are direct exchanges focused on business issues. Personal chitchat is often secondary or nonexistent. In other cultures, the social interaction is a vital part of business relationships. This creates a problem for salespeople in North America when they actually gain opportunities to have those social moments because they are unprepared. They view the social interactions as casual exchanges bearing little or no relevance to the larger business dialogue. There is, however, a strategy to use during seemingly casual exchanges that establishes the authority Cialdini identified as necessary to build credibility and influence.

At the dining table prior to the actual business dialogue, the buyer might casually share information about family, hobbies, or other personal interests. The unprepared salesperson uses that moment to respond casually without considering the strategic opportunity to establish authority. In between the casual dialogue about families, interests, and hobbies, the salesperson can introduce stories that boost credibility. Cialdini writes, "Expose your expertise; don't assume it's self-evident."

Noah wondered, "How do I prove to my clients that I'm better than the competition?"

Abe quoted Cialdini and said, "Expose your expertise."

"How do I do that without a 'sales diploma' that says I'm good at my job?" Noah asked.

"You can do two things, one of which works not as well as the other," Abe said. "Most salespeople learn to deliver an elevator speech. Have you heard of that?"

Noah rolled his eyes and Abe laughed.

"Exactly!" said Abe. "Bragging does no good. During your conversations with clients, share stories of success you have had with other clients. The easy stories to remember are those during which you helped a client with a product issue. I'd love for you to dig deeper and share stories where you have consulted with your clients unselfishly. Tell stories of ways you've helped your business-to-business clients without making a sale."

Noah again squinted his eyes in thought. Abe patiently let him have his moment.

"I'm not sure I can think of any off the top of my head," Noah admitted.

"I'm not surprised," Abe said. "It's why you are struggling to discover the reasons to schedule the next meeting in relationships, which we call 'the next step.' Right?"

Noah nodded.

"We need you to learn the right things to know about your client. Understand more and you'll easily figure the next steps in the business relationship process."

Noah said, "I don't see how those go together."

Abe said, "Let's recap. You told me you were struggling to find the purpose to set up the *next meeting* with a client during the existing sales call, right?"

Noah nodded, "Yes."

Abe reminded Noah that he had asked, "'What are the things I need to know about my client to figure out these next steps?'"

"Oh! Yes," Noah said as he remembered the question. "But I was thinking about how to make a sale, not how I can help my clients without making a sale. I'm not sure I know how or even if I could."

Abe let that comment linger and Noah got a little uncomfortable.

"Maybe you can't," Abe said.

Closing Influence Is Relational before Transactional

Noah sat silently and realized he was being baited. "So are you going to give me the answer or not?" Noah asked with a mix of embarrassment, openness, and humor.

Abe enjoyed the energy of his willing student and said, "We don't close deals in our business; we open relationships. You are thinking about the transaction instead of the relationship. You are thinking about creating an exchange of consideration. Do you know what consideration is?"

Noah said, "I guess it's a kind of courtesy, right?"

Abe kindly smiled and said, "It can be, but that's not what it means in legalese. In business relationships, consideration is a legal term and it means money or an exchange of goods in a contractual relationship. In fact, I'd rather you thought of business courtesy as the key to increasing your success rather than consideration.

"The 'close' of the sale," Abe continued, "is based not as much on the agreed transactional details as it is on the trust and credibility you bring to the table. If people trust you and know you're knowledgeable, then you have authority. You asked me how to prove you're better than the competition, right?"

"Yes, I did."

Abe said, "Authority. It doesn't come on a piece of paper. It doesn't come on a business card. We both know it doesn't come from an elevator speech. It comes when people believe you are the one who is in the best position to help them succeed. Makes sense?"

"Yes," said Noah leaning forward to absorb his mentor's words.

"Good," Abe said. "We'll hit the road on some calls together next week and discuss it. Sound like a good plan to you?"

Noah smiled and said, "Sounds great!"

14

The Value of Business Relationships

The Deferral of Self-Interest

Abe rode with Noah on joint sales calls as he had done for years with salespeople. The coaching protocols are simple. Observe quietly. Interject to correct an error. Demonstrate skills when appropriate. After each interaction, Abe replays the meeting with his pupil as a means to improve behavioral sales economic awareness and tactics. At the conclusion of a full session of multiple meetings, Abe delivers constructive praise and feedback to help the performer improve.

In the middle of the day, Abe explained to Noah that the meetings he scheduled were excellent. He was able to use the ten-point scorecard (Figure 12.6) as a method to evaluate objectively the value of each meeting. Abe noted, however, that the content of Noah's meetings could be improved with better listening skills.

"Your intention is focused on the sale instead of the client," Abe noted.

"Well, yes," Noah admitted. "That's how I make money."

Abe chuckled and said, "I must politely disagree. Your pay is calculated by the level of sales and profitability you create. The *how you make money part* is determined by the level to which you can help your customers succeed. Sales excellence requires the *deferral of self-interest.*"

Noah wondered what that meant. He was driving and trying to concentrate while also defending his performance. He mentioned that Abe had jumped into the previous meeting to illustrate a "softer" approach to selling. Abe corrected Noah and said, "I wasn't illustrating a softer approach. I was demonstrating an *interested* approach. I was showing you how you can truly understand your client without focusing entirely on the outcome of a sale. Remember how we spoke earlier about the 'feeling' you had about a good meeting?"

"Yes," said Noah while proudly recollecting the enlightened and complimentary conversation he had with Abe.

"I want your feeling to now extend beyond the outcomes for you and focus on the client," Abe said. "In that last meeting, you heard me ask the buyer about her business. I wondered how she acquired her sales leads. We discussed that problem she had hiring people briefly. Do you recall?"

Noah nodded.

"I did that for you, not her. I want you to see what a good dialogue looks like when you are truly engaging the client."

Noah agreed that the dialogue interested her, but didn't really result in a sale or even a follow-up meeting. "I get that you are looking for a lot of specific information, but I just don't see what we are supposed to do with it."

Abe said, "Maybe just show we're interested. Maybe more. Maybe less. We'll see."

Noah drove. He didn't like disappointing his mentor and the moments of silence distressed him for a bit. They pulled up to the Starbucks at the strip mall to meet Noah's customer, a remodeling contractor working from his pickup truck while managing his business from his home. Noah presented the price his customer requested and provided the product brochure necessary to promote the goods to the contractor's customer, the homeowner. Then the conversation digressed into personal areas while Abe was conspicuously silent.

Noah was relieved when Abe jumped in to ask, "Mind if I ask how you price your services?"

The heavyset contractor, wearing a t-shirt with his logo and soiled jeans, said he figured out how much labor it would take him and charged by the hour. He gave his customers a guesstimate to the number of hours it would take. "No markup on the products?" Abe asked.

"No. Not really."

"No markup on your time?" Abe asked.

"Nope. Just the hourly rate. My customers can be pretty demanding about prices," he said to justify his methodology.

"I hear that!" Abe said to ensure his salesman's customer was not put on the defensive. "That being said, I've had the privilege of working with a lot of people like you. A lot of contractors have shared insights into their business and I can tell you how they price their services a little differently…that is, if you're interested."

Predictably, Abe had some valuable insights for the

contractor. He reminded him that he used tools that cost money and sooner or later they would need to be replaced. "It's also true about your truck," he added. "You also spend time preparing proposals for customers and taking time to find new leads. I suspect you need to also take care of your accounting books."

"Yes. At night," the contractor said.

Abe smiled and said, "Accountants and bookkeepers are a cost of business also. Even if you don't pay them directly there is a time cost that is associated with it and, more importantly, your competitors in the market are charging for many of the things you're not."

The contractor nodded. Abe concluded with a simple suggestion, "You might not believe this, but most contractors charge a markup on products as well as a flat burden rate on capital and labor.

"Burden is the markup," Abe said. "It's the rate at which indirect costs are included in the price of a project. So, a project might have direct labor costs and material costs. But hidden costs include marketing expenses, sales costs, accounting time, equipment depreciation, and more. A business can't be profitable without subsidizing the foundation of the business operation. Most successful contractor includes them. In fact there is a book about it.

"Here," Abe said, while pulling out his business card. "This is the name of the book." Abe wrote down on his business card *The Remodelers Guide to Making and Managing Money*, a book by Linda Case. "Order this one," he concluded. "It will help you. I'm concerned for you that you're only getting paid as an employee while taking all the risk as a business owner."

The silent contractor was staring and hanging on to every word Abe delivered. It dawned on Noah that his customer didn't have a pen or paper. Noah wish he had been taking notes for him, but was happy that the book recommendation eventually was offered.

As they drove silently, Noah spied the grin on Abe's face. "You must be awfully proud of yourself," Noah said with a chuckle.

"Oh no. Not at all," Abe said. "What makes you think I would be?"

"Because of what happened in there," Noah said.

"Did something happen?" Abe asked.

Noah laughed and said, "You know it did. I get it."

Abe softly said, "Good. Tell me. Tell me what you got."

Noah said, "You really helped that guy. He needs it. I'm worried he won't take the advice or do anything about it."

Abe said, "People surprise you. He might. He said he'd buy the book."

"He did," said Noah. They drove silently for a few moments and Noah said, "There is a problem. He probably wants you to be his salesman instead of me. Now you'll have to come with me every time I see him!"

Abe laughed and said, "Or we could give you the same skills so that you can repeat the performance with him and others. How about that?"

"I like that idea."

"Think that buyer will want to buy more from us after that meeting?" Abe asked.

"Maybe," Noah said. "He'll want you to come back."

"Or you," Abe said. "If you can develop the right skills to

consult with your clients. Did you notice that my interaction with him had nothing to do with our company, our products, or our services?"

"Yes," said Noah. "I did."

"That's what we'll call the deferral of self-interest. Your customer knows what you want. You know what you want. Everyone knows. You want a sale. But if you can defer your attention from that and focus on ways to help your client succeed, you'll get plenty of opportunities to sell. Remember that *the how you make money* part is enhanced by *the deferral of self-interest*. Reduce your expectation of personal gain and increase your intention to help. That is when people figure out ways to do business with you. Got it?"

"Got it!" Noah said as they drove down the highway to the next meeting.

You Behave What You Believe

Abe commented to Noah, "You said, 'maybe.'"

"I did? When?" Noah asked.

"I asked if you thought that guy would want to buy more from us after that meeting and you said, 'maybe.'"

"Yes," Noah said. "I did say that."

"I believe he will. You aren't sure. You behave what you believe," Abe said before asking, "What did you see in that meeting with the contractor?"

"Well," Noah said. "I saw that you helped him a lot, but we didn't get the next meeting. But it was still great. There was no next step though."

Abe said, "As a follow-up to that meeting, I suspect your customer would have been happy for me to meet him again and provide some sales advice. He would have enjoyed a referral to another noncompeting contractor who could share ideas. There were opportunities I could have fulfilled, but didn't want to put you on the spot by committing your time to something you're not ready for.

"I wanted to demonstrate a different skill for you there. I wanted you to get out of your mindset of self-interest. Self-interest is in our human nature and selling to businesses makes it all too easy to concentrate on that," Abe said.

"I believe I do a great job of helping my clients and not focusing on myself," Noah said without a hint of defensiveness. He believed, like most salespeople, that his intention and behaviors were consistently directed toward his clients' best interests.

Abe calmly said, "How do you do that?"

Noah wasn't sure. He felt he probably didn't have the answer Abe was looking for, but believed nevertheless that he had a great answer and told Abe, "I make myself available to my customers, provide good service, and do it at a fair price."

"Everyone says that. It makes them good product providers if they actually do it, although many don't. So you are definitely ahead of the average. But you want to be way above average, right?"

Noah said, "I do for sure."

Abe said, "Remember when you handed a price to one of our customers a few months ago? You said, 'Do me a favor and let me know how our price looks after you've reviewed all your quotes.'"

Noah remembered the lesson and said, "I know. I might as well have begged him to negotiate with me because my gestures and words promised the buyer there was room to move."

"That's true, but not the lesson here," Abe said. "The reason it was about pricing for you is because you didn't see how you and our products fit into the bigger picture. You didn't convert the conversation to the profits. You *behaved* as if the sale was about competitive pricing, not profits…even if you didn't feel like you *believed* it."

"What does that mean?" asked Noah.

"It means your beliefs must be reflected in your behaviors. Your customer can buy our products from a lot of people. The moment you said you wanted to know where we stand as a price comparison to the competition, your behavior tacitly implied that it is about pricing and that we're similar to the competition. You say that you help your customers as you expressed belief, but your behavior shows you fear being price competitive?"

Noah nodded.

Abe said, "If your delivery can save your customers money by reducing labor, does that make them more profitable?"

Noah nodded.

"If you can avoid errors to guarantee complete deliveries, does that make you more valuable than a competitive salesperson who makes mistakes on orders?"

Noah nodded.

"Those two issues illustrate how you help your customer manage costs. Don't just believe it. Behave it," Abe said. "There is more. I was showing you, with that last contractor, how to make more money by running his business better. I believe, because I have experienced it, that buyers become more loyal to me when I do things like that. That contractor could stand a lot of advice he might not take. My goal wasn't to help the contractor there, although I hope I did. It was to illustrate for you how to align your behaviors and beliefs to help customers succeed.

"It's not just about pricing. It's about caring. It's about professionalism. It's about the sales process. Your beliefs drive your behaviors. If you believe business success is about likeability and friendship than you risk becoming unprofessional at the wrong moments by shifting your behaviors. If you believe, as you stated earlier, that you get paid for sales and not for helping people, you will behave that way. Just *believe* that helping means more than just being a good supplier. It means adding your personal value, something your customers can get only from *you*. Make sense?"

"Got it," Noah said. He realized he was promising a knowing mentor to fulfill a role he wasn't sure he could. He had always been trying make sales, first and foremost. He had a powerful lesson to learn.

The Deferral of Self-Interest

G – General (WIFT)
O – Opportunity (WIFM)

Figure 14.1: *Opportunity* is the pursuit of information about products and services provided by the salesperson. The selfish salesperson tunes into to WIFM—*What's in It for Me? General* discovery and listening centers around the challenge of the buyer where the salesperson tunes into WIFT—*What's in It for Them?* The leap of belief puts general discovery first with the faith that helping clients succeed ultimately results in more organic opportunity for sales.

Abe pulled out a piece of paper (Figure 14.1) and said, "The salesperson's instinct is to determine as quickly as possible any *opportunity* for a sale. Ironically, the path to creating a sale often comes by relinquishing the desire for immediate results in favor of seeking a *general* understanding of the buyer. Resist the desire for immediate gain. The buyer will engage more consistently when you understand their larger challenges."

Noah nodded and prepared for the rest of the lesson.

Go for More

In business, the two ways a company builds profitability are increasing topline results and reducing bottom line costs. It's that simple. The salesperson who can enhance customer profitability, in the business-to-business relationship, becomes the preferred supplier of choice.

Topline profitability is enhanced by lead acquisition, sales processes, marketing strategies, and market challenges. Bottom line expenses are controlled by operational efficiencies, labor management, and cost control. The success for the buyer's business is accomplished with a team of people working in unison. Finally, the buyer is an individual who possesses the same dreams, fears, and challenges like others in the workplace. The salesperson who taps into these categories of understanding gains a marked competitive edge.

Abe took out another piece of paper and said, "Let's not start with opportunity," he said. "Let's put *general* discovery first. Let's understand how our customers and prospects *market and sell* their services; let's understand how they *operate* to manage costs and efficiencies; let's discover how *relationships* work inside the organization; let's feel the challenge of the individual by tapping into *ego*."

Abe finished writing and turned the paper to Noah while saying, "Let's GO for MORE than our competition. Let's listen better. If we understand more, it will become the core of our competitive edge. What do you think?"

Noah said, "I've seen it in action. I also see how this will lead to more next steps."

"How?" asked Abe.

"Well," Noah said. "First I'm going to buy that book you recommended to the contractor and see what ideas I can share with my customers to help them run their business better. I'm also going to schedule meetings to have people show me how their business works to make sure we order and deliver to them properly. I am also going to schedule time to meet coworkers inside companies. I'm definitely going to make sure to invite my customers and prospects to our office so they can meet people here. There are a few ways I see and I'm sure more will appear if I keep looking for them."

"Perfect," said Abe. "That's the key. Be on the lookout for ways to help and then schedule appointments. The more your practice, the better you'll be. It all begins by understanding your customer."

```
┌─────────────────────────────────────────┐
│                                           │
│              GO for MORE                  │
│                                           │
│     G – General Information               │
│          M – Marketing and Sales          │
│          O – Operations                    │
│          R – Relationships                  │
│          E – Ego                            │
│                                           │
│     O – Opportunity Information            │
│          Who? What? Why? Weaknesses?      │
│                                           │
└─────────────────────────────────────────┘
```

Figure 14.2: Effective listening starts by understanding the buyer's situation in business-to-business (B-2-B) selling. This means discover how the buyer *markets* products and services as well as the *operational* challenges to make the business work profitably. Every organization is made up of individuals to form team *relationships*. Most notably, the salesperson must dig to understand the motivations, obstacles, and influence of the individual buyer's ego.

Abe created a new piece of paper and added the letters M, O, R, and E under *general* information. He scribbled a few words after each letter and added a few key words underneath the section for *opportunity* information. He turned the paper to Noah and said, "Take everything I'm about to tell you with skepticism. I don't want you to believe me until you've tried it. After that, let me know what you think."

Abe proceeded to explain a listening system designed specifically for business-to-business sales. He noted that information is the key to deepening business-to-business relationships, particularly if the salesperson is sincerely interested in helping the customer profit. The experience of two copier salespeople in the previous chapter proved that success is not about perfectly crafted questions, although a well-phrased question never hurts. The question doesn't matter unless it gets the right information and is actually heard.

There isn't a single human being who has not gone into bobblehead mode at some point in their lives. The person you are speaking with is telling you something very vital about their life and you suddenly realize that, in spite of the eye contact and bobbling head of acknowledgement you offer empathetically, you haven't heard a word the person says. You panic because you may have to respond to something said and won't have a clue what to say. In a second your mind moves away from that train of thought and you wonder if the person realizes you're not listening when that thought is replaced with a new panic attack that you're still not listening!

Listening is an act of caring. It means being present for the sake of understanding the situation, challenges, and dreams of another person. No agenda. No personal gain. The practice provides numerous benefits for the listener, particularly in business. One benefit is the power of reciprocity, a proven factor of influence according to Robert Cialdini. It is a universal trait in all humanity that we want to repay good deeds. The salesperson who listens gains the willingness of the buyer to listen in return. The second benefit is the business education acquired from the buyer. As the buyer illustrates their methods for acquiring leads, selling, marketing, managing labor, and utilizing resources, the salesperson gains lessons in creating profit. The third benefit is a result of the second. The more business lessons obtained, the more likely it is for the salesperson to discover consultative sales opportunities above and beyond the price and delivery of a product.

Here is a powerful outline to discover what you can learn about your prospects and clients to become a more effective supplier and contributor to their success.

M = Marketing and Sales

It has often been said that nothing happens until a sale is made. A salesperson should know this truth as well as anyone in the business world. There is nothing to produce, no people to hire, no buyer to sell...until someone makes a sale. This means that the first objective is to understand how the client acquires new business, a process that can take the seller into a deep conversation that endures throughout the duration of the relationship.

Important factors to understand include the ways in which the client advertises and acquires customers. If the client has a sales staff, it would benefit the salesperson to understand how the client manages the sales staff, establishes goals, and measures performance. Each business, even when selling similar products or services, can target different market niches, geographies, and demographics. Deep understanding means discovering the buyer's competitive challenges and means to differentiate from their competition. The salesperson should recognize that a higher price can be justified when presented in the larger context of increased profits through better markup or higher sales volume for the client.

Here is a list of twenty-one things to know about your business clients' sales and marketing challenges:

MARKETING

1. What products and services do they provide?
2. How does your customer get leads?
3. Who is their target audience?
4. How do they advertise?

5. What is their geographic coverage?
6. What future growth plans does the company have?
7. How do they communicate to their audience with social media or other electronic means?
8. How do they manage customer information?
9. What are their competitive challenges?
10. How do they differentiate from their competition?
11. What other marketing challenges does the company have in their own words (e.g., fear of new competitors entering the market, economic conditions)?

SALES

12. What is the sale structure? How many salespeople? Mangers? Executives?
13. What are the sales goals for the individuals? For the company?
14. What are the company's pricing strategies and philosophy?
15. How is sales performance measured and tracked?
16. Does the company have a defined sales process?
17. How does the company onboard and train new salespeople?
18. How does the company upsell?
19. Upselling
20. Margin Management
21. What other sales challenges does the company have in their own words (e.g., aging sales force, difficulty with accountability)?

O = Operations

Marketing and sales provide the income, but without operational efficiency, profits are lost. The astute salesperson recognizes that there are processes that successful companies develop to succeed. The costs of running a successful business include fixed, variable, and product costs. Fixed costs include the capital to run the business such as buildings, computers, transportation, and machinery. Variable costs include salaries, insurance, overtime, and other labor costs. Material costs include the products the salesperson is promoting to the buyer.

Somewhere in this lesson description, a salesperson starts to wonder if it is really necessary to know all this about a customer's business. The short answer is yes. The salesperson should recognize that the price delivered can be justified when presented in the larger context of operational efficiencies and reduced long-term costs. The total cost of goods is always more than the price.

Here is a list of ten things to know about your business clients' operational challenges:

22. How does the company manage project/product flow?
23. Inventory practices and challenges?
24. How does the company acquire and onboard new employees?
25. How does the company manage labor costs?
26. How does the company manage customer fulfillment (e.g., deliveries, scheduling)?
27. How does the company manage product order processing?

28. What insurance and regulation challenges face the company?
29. What impact does seasonal demand place on the company?
30. What are the accounting and financial challenges of the company (e.g., profits, cash flow)?
31. What other operational challenges are affecting the company (e.g., succession planning, future sale of the company)?

R = Relationships

There is an old saying that says it's not what you know, but who you know. In the age of Yelp and Google reviews, it is no longer who you know that matters most. It is who knows you. We live in an age of reputation and one-star to five-star ratings. Being known is as important as knowing. Almost every salesperson in his or her career has lost an account when a key contact left the organization. The best solution is to prevent a potential break in relations by establishing *depth of relationship* with intention.

Depth of relationship means knowing numerous participants in the organization. The astute salesperson recognizes that the worker bee of today in an organization is a high-level leader tomorrow. Thus, the relationships fostered widely across the organization enable the salesperson to succeed in the short term and stabilize the relationship over the long haul.

Decisions are rarely made by a single person. Notwithstanding the trite advice so often given to "get to the decision-maker," the real world of business-to-business is filled with committees and multiple people affected by and affecting the vendor-buyer relationship. An operations manager may be the one who tells the purchasing manager that deliveries are not coming in as planned. A salesperson might complain about the product quality from a vendor. A seemingly unimportant receptionist, too often referred to as a "gatekeeper," might actually be a highly influential player on the buyer's team. Good selling means understanding how the entire organization works and striving to become viewed as an "unpaid employee" on the team.

Here is a list of seven things to know about your business clients' operational challenges:

32. What is the organization flow chart for the company? Can you draw it?
33. How many people do you know in the company?
34. How many people know you?
35. How are decisions made in the organization (e.g., consensus, top-down)?
36. What are the organizational politics (i.e., internal, who wields influence)?
37. Culture and values (e.g., open, dictatorial, spiritual, partying, etc.)?
38. If your main contact(s) left the company tomorrow, how stable is your relationship?

E = Ego

The Mackay 66 provides a powerful list of details the salesperson can know about a buyer. With all due respect to a man I admire greatly, I would assert that it is incomplete and slightly misdirected in the modern age. Nearly every aspect of the list describes information about a single buyer. Ideally it would be wonderful to have a detailed profile not only of the main influencer in an organization, but all staff members. The sixty-six items enable the salesperson to develop incredibly strong rapport with a single individual.

The list is incomplete because it does not detail the deeper aspects of a client's challenges. In fact, it implies for the reader (even if Mr. Mackay didn't intend it) that business relationships are like friendships. We've already dispelled the notion that friendships are the foundation of business relationships. Furthermore, it presumes that a line of discovery about a person's personal interests is the key to building personal rapport.

The modern age is a time of tension and overwhelmingness. People don't have extra time on their hands. The salesperson who gets right to business may actually have a competitive advantage to the salesperson who opens a meeting with idle chitchat. The old notion that each sales meeting should start with a human-interest dialogue is passé.

Thus the fourth category to emphasize in listening includes the *ego*. In this case, the ego is not in reference to egotism and selfishness. Instead it is more about understanding *career* challenges from the buyer's perspective as empathetically as possible. The objective of business connection is to develop mutual advocacy where associates discover ways to help each other succeed in their careers.

The astute salesperson understands that the buyer has a lot more to consider than the transaction and relationship with the salesperson. There is job pressure from superiors; career fears and aspirations; competencies and fears of incompetency. There is a human being, not just an interaction to manage. Help people succeed and grow and they will help you. Here is a list of seven things to know about ways individuals succeed on the job:

39. How does the person do his or her job?
40. What is their personality style (e.g., analytical, insecure, demanding, egocentric)?
41. What are the individual's career goals (e.g., growth, stability, retirement)?
42. How much power does the buyer wield in the organization (e.g., facilitator, leader)?
43. What is the buyer's advocacy level (i.e., do they support or block you)?
44. Fears and aspirations (e.g., job loss, promotion, their boss getting fired)?
45. What other personal aspects of their career or life are important?

The Other "O" = Opportunity

The purpose of GO for MORE is to help the salesperson consciously recognize the power in changing listening frequencies. Instead of tuning into WIFM, *what's in it for me*, the successful salesperson understands the buyer's world, WIFT, or *what's in it for them*. The dialogue and, more importantly, sincere interest to understand the buyer's world earns the salesperson the reciprocal *opportunity* to determine what products and services could be a fit.

Reciprocity, as noted, is a proven key to influence. Robert Cialdini, a Stanford psychologist, ran experiments on factors of influence published in his book *Influence*. He found that reciprocity was a powerful motivator of human behavior. It is something that many people experience with their friends when fighting over a bill at dinner. One diner says, "I got this one." The other then quickly reaches toward the waiter to intercept the check while saying, "No way. This one's on me." Then the debate starts as both diners argue to *pay* for a meal that the other is offering for free. It's a curious example of behavioral economics at work driven by the power of reciprocity.

The ultimate winner is the one who says, "You bought pizzas at the house the other night. It's my turn." The other combatant in the fight for the bill relents with the caveat that he will get the next one. The deal is agreed; the bill is paid; and the next time the two dine, the same argument will ensue because the law of reciprocity is so strong in humans, well other than the diner with the proverbial "alligator arms," that most of us want to pay our debts. We want to reciprocate gestures of kindness and generosity.

This is how the GO for MORE works, too. The salesperson who first tunes into the buyer's *general* challenges, without even realizing it, builds up a cache of reciprocity that will soon enable the salesperson to obtain information about the *opportunities* that both the buyer and seller know is the true motivation of the salesperson.

Here is a list of five things to know about a potential sales opportunity:

46. What products and services that you supply are of interest to your buyer?
47. Who has the buyer shopped with or currently buying from?
48. Why? What are the competitor's strengths?
49. What are the competitor's weaknesses?
50. What have you learned in GO for MORE that makes you a fit for the client?

The KRI of Relationships

The KPIs of business relationships are the amount of knowledge you know about the client's *business*. It's helpful, without question, to know hobbies, spouse's names, birthdates, and other personal information. It's vital to understand how the business is run.

The KRI of sales success is the share of purchases you get from a buyer in the categories you sell. The third party benefit administrator can count the total products available in their portfolio and cross reference with the client's buying practices to determine *customer share*, which is *the percentage of business the supplier earns of the product categories available for purchase from a client*. The lumber dealer can determine that the available total package of lumber, windows, doors, and other products add up to $50,000 on an average home. If that were the case and the builder purchases lumber and windows only for an average of $30,000 per home, then the supplier would be earning a 60% customer share.

The benefit of skilled relationship development is customer share. The real power of listening is influence and unbreakable customer loyalty.

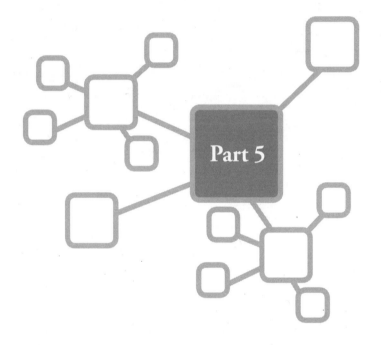

Part 5

MACROSALES
ECONOMICS

15

Zip-Whoosh and an Intro to Macrosales Economics

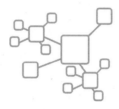

Nobody Plans to Fail

Picture a group of very large teenagers, many in excess of three hundred muscular pounds, expelling the energy of youth with shouts and shoves inside a lecture room. This is the picture painted by Brad Williams, the vice president of sales for a Canadian manufacturer of flooring. It's not the picture of his sales meeting, but the picture of a media center one week before a big football game.

Years earlier, Lou Holtz sat in Brad's California living room to recruit him as a defensive end for the Fighting Irish of Notre Dame, an offer Williams accepted. Today he leverages his football experience as a metaphor for the KPIs of individual performance and their link to long-term success for individuals as well as organizations. He shared the enlightening story of his experience with me a few years ago.

"The door opens ten minutes prior to the start of the meeting," Williams says. "Every team member is already seated in place, because the coach has made it clear they are late if not ten minutes early."

Williams said, due to the esteem his players hold for Coach Holtz, the room instantly goes silent and all eyes look forward as the man of mighty influence walks into the room and starts to speak. He assures his team they will win the upcoming game if each performer commits to three KPIs.

Williams defined the KPIs. "One: each player is expected to cover his assignment. Two: each player must outhit his man. Three: we will commit less turnovers than our opponent. If you do these three things, Coach Holtz assures a win." It was that simple and pretty hard to argue with the success of the man who restored greatness to the Notre Dame football tradition.

Success is about the results, of course. But without a performance game plan, there is nothing to do. KPIs predict KRIs and without them, success is accidental. Success requires carefully calculated performance, even if that performance is as simple as three little metrics. Cover your assignment; outhit your man; commit less turnovers; win an NCAA football championship.

It's a cliché, but still a good one: *Nobody plans to fail; they fail to plan.* The plan fails because KPIs are ignored.

Talent Is Average

One of the truths about salespeople, and performers in any field, is that the total pool of talent is average. Sum up the top performers, average performers, poor performers, and everyone in between; then divide by the total. The end result is that talent is average. It is this aspect of Lou Holtz's career that makes his performance admirable.

His track record includes a series of tenures that began when he consistently took over mediocre teams and quickly turned them into contenders. The North Carolina State Wolfpack was 3-8 in 1971, 8-3 in 1972 under first-year coach Lou Holtz. The South Carolina team was 1-10 the year he took over and, after a single transition season, he led the team to an 8-4 record and a ranking in the top twenty teams of the NCAA. Same talent; different results. He turned around a team that had been struggling for years at Notre Dame and led the team to the national football championship in three years.

It was his experience at Arkansas that might be the most impressive. He took over a team that, in 1977, that had lost half of its games. The next year he led that team to an 11-1 record, which is only a small part of the story. At the Orange Bowl, the Arkansas Razorbacks faced the heavily favored Oklahoma Sooners, the team that would become the national champion if they won that game.

If the odds against an Arkansas victory weren't slim enough, Holtz benched three of his top players for disciplinary reasons just prior to the game. Two of those players had scored nearly 80% of the team's points that season. In spite of being an eighteen-point underdog and losing those three players,

Holtz's squad won the game 31-6. *Less* talent; better outcomes.

As a consultant to clients and a well-connected leader in my industry, I am frequently asked if I know a good sales candidate for hire. The tacit objective is to find a prepackaged success story, which saves the organization and managers the task of training and development. I've never understood why leaders think it's better (or easier) to hire skills away from the competition. Success means building your own results system. Besides, the pool of talent is average. The difference between winning and losing is not talent; it's the performance plan. *Good planning with average talent beats great talent with no planning.*

In the late 1970s and early 1980s, the Pittsburgh Steelers won four Super Bowls under the leadership of Hall of Fame coach Chuck Knoll. I was a big fan of the Steelers in those days, a team with eight future Hall of Fame players. I can't verify whether or not this is the most Hall of Fame players ever to be on one team at the same time, but it would seem a good bet. The point is that it's a rarity to have that many Hall of Famers on any team in any endeavor, including sales.

Since that time, I have come to believe that those eight players may have *become* Hall of Fame stars not because they were necessarily more gifted than their competitors. I think it had everything to do with Chuck Knoll and his performance leadership. It's possible that the Steelers just lucked out and drafted the best players, but the odds are against it. Performers are defined by their performance; performance is coached by leaders. The Steelers were the NFL dynasty of envy until the New England Patriots, under the leadership of Bill Belichick, became the all-time leader in Super Bowl victories.

The success of the Patriots has become, for me, the evidence that Hall of Fame superstars are not just born; they are made and coached. Belichick has managed to create a perennial winner at a time when league parity is enforced specifically to prevent dynasties and cycle interest in all football markets by keeping as many teams relevant as possible. Some might argue that having the greatest quarterback of all time helps. Others might argue he doesn't even have the greatest quarterback of his time. I argue that his quarterback, Tom Brady, will be regarded *because* he played for the team with a plan. Who knows?

One quarterback contributes to a dynasty. A team builds it, particularly when led by a leader with a plan. Belichick's plan is famous and simple: "Do your job."

Zip-Whoosh

The reason the Patriots kept on winning is not because of better talent, although they have very gifted players. The talent has changed so much over the years that it virtually proves Belichick's skills at coordinating the right performance. This was clarified for me during a game not involving the Patriots.

A receiver for my Michigan Wolverines, the guy who catches passes from the quarterback, *zipped* five yards straight down the field and then quickly cut to the middle. After making the cut, he recognized he was wide open to receive a pass and waved at the quarterback. The wave caused the receiver to slow down and, in that time, a defender caught up and knocked the ball down as it was about to hit the receiver's hands. The announcer pointed out that the mistake was not on the quarterback, but on the receiver who slowed down. The receiver needed to keep running at full speed and let the pass hit him in stride. That's when it hit me. He needed to do his job and let the quarterback do his.

His went *zip*, but he didn't *whoosh*. That's what I call that play, the *zip-whoosh*. Zip down five yards and whoosh across the middle of the field. The receiver who slowed down is a very talented performer, fast and strong. Being a good performer, however, is not enough. Performers are individuals laced with talent, some more than others. The performance is the thing that players do with that talent, some better than others.

It made me think of Wes Welker, a former a star with the New England Patriots. Welker was the master of the *zip-whoosh*. A few hundred plays in his career consist of zipping five yards and quickly cutting through the middle where he received the ball in stride from the quarterback. No hand waving. No slowing down. He did the job as prescribed at full speed.

Welker is gone now. He has been replaced with a new performer, Julian Edelman. Edelman and Welker are both relatively small by professional football standards, but equally quick on their feet. They possess similar talents, although talent and size are secondary to the story. Edelman has replaced Welker and, with equal competence to his predecessor in the role of Patriot receiver, perfectly executes the *zip-whoosh*. Different performers; same performance. It's a trademark Belichick practice: find the right performers and get them to *do their jobs*.

The one thing a salesperson or organization can know is that talent is not enough. Anders Ericsson proved it in *Peak* by defining how Alexander Alekhine became the greatest chess player in the world by studious practice and repetitive performance. He backs up his story by illustrating how concert violinists, Olympic swimmers, and other peak performers achieve success. They practice the *performance* repeatedly.

Here is the question every salesperson and organization must ask: Are you measuring to the performance or the results?

The Proving Ground

The formula to "test and observe," then later engage in "proactive consciousness" offers process to develop and test the skills of selling. It is the process of sales economics where individual behaviors can be linked to short-term outcomes. It's easy because you can instantly determine whether or not a single behavior produces the desired outcome. You can quickly verify that an appointment yields better results than a cold call. It's easy to test the bid avoidance presentation and determine its results instantly. A salesperson only needs to learn once that the law of holding your price sometimes enables you to get it.

Long-term goals are different. They require a level of tracking and observation that is simple, but not easy. This is the subject for *macrosales economics* (MaSE), which requires a different level of analysis and commitment to achieve long-term results. As an example, the measurement for the quality of sales call is an excellent example of a MiSE concept. That being said, the true effectiveness of the measurement can only be ascertained in the larger analysis of long-term performance. That is, one sales call by any measurement can be lucky; hundreds of sales calls reveal a trend and correlation between performance and results.

MaSE provides the larger picture analysis of sales performance by expanding the concept of an individual sales call into a larger picture of calendar management. MaSE provides the measurement foundation to achieve long-term sales goals with meaningful KPIs that link to desired KRIs. Lastly, a measurement theory on networking earlier introduced as *transactional advocacy* will be reinvestigated to help create more transactional dependability in business-to-business relationships.

There is powerful evidence that supports proper planning and development of KPIs. Suppose the Steelers did manage to "out-talent" every other team in football and were destined for greatness solely on the shoulders of a Hall of Fame squad even without a game plan. Bill Belichick has proven he can out-manage every other coach in spite of a league that is calculated to establish, and almost enforce, team parity; it is possible he has been the beneficiary of more talent than his opponents, but it seems unlikely. Lou Holtz has proven with certainty that a better game plan with same talent than his predecessors produces better long-term results.

All evidence points to the power of a game plan that can be provided, in the sales profession, with MaSE data. If you have made it this far, keep going. There is a plan and it is going to get exciting!

16

Calendar Management: The Glue of Sales Success

The Test of Ability and Willingness

The earlier story of Noah's ten-point sales call illustrated how everything can go right in a sales call, even if it seems unlikely. The sales call measurement is more than a fictitious portrayal of sales excellence at work. The quality of a sales call has been tested as a KPI that is predictive as a relative measure of competence. The research has taken place with numerous salespeople whose performances were observed and measured to produce consistent correlations between KPIs and KRIs.

The process begins by inviting salespeople to accept personal coaching. The selected salespeople are asked to plan a full day of activity for the coach to observe during a ride along session. Think of it as a golf pro not merely working with a student in the practice area, but instead watching the golfer during the entire round of actual play; instead of rehearsing scripts and processes in the training room, this is an observation of live sales performance. The performer is instructed specifically to *plan the perfect day*.

A perfect day includes a specified number of sales calls with the intention that they are made as scheduled appointments. Depending on the geography, product, and industry, a fair allowance for cold calls and warm calls can be tossed in. Ideally the salesperson should know the success factors include appointments, discovering new leads, deepening relationships by meeting new contacts, and creating follow-up plans during meetings. For this reason, a successful coaching session requires advanced notice to permit proper preparation by the salesperson.

I have prepared salespeople for the exercise with the suggestion that they "fool me." They are encouraged to make the day better than any day in their career as a means to trick me into believing it is what they do every day. They are told to cheat if necessary and use every means to create success with one caveat. The day must include a number of interactions with prospects and salespeople can't make social visits to existing customers merely for the sake of filling in time. Prospects must be included to prove the salesperson can generate new sales from scratch; social visits to existing clients can't count because they are counterproductive.

The advanced notice to plan the perfect day is required for a very logical reason. *If the salesperson can't produce a high-quality performance with advanced notice, under the scrutiny of a watching eye, there is little chance it will happen when the no one is observing.* This is a valuable coaching exercise for both veteran salespeople and entry-level performers designed to assess their *ability* and *willingness*. It is the test that determines sales *ability* to build a single day of quality in the field. It is also a test of *willingness* to see if they will even try. Can they or can't they? Will they or won't they? Those are the questions.

Some managers might argue that a surprise inspection is their best way to determine what a salesperson *really* does when nobody is looking. This might be a logical method in some circumstances such as a corrective action for a deficient performer after adequate training and coaching has occurred, but is not suitable for this exercise of benchmarking. This approach would be as foolish as the head football coach never instructing the players and then showing up for a surprise practice inspection. Chances for success would be low.

Notice the exercise centers on prospecting and calendar management exclusively. Other selling skills can be evaluated, but are not the main emphasis during the initial coaching and observation session. Again think of coaching lessons in other endeavors. A piano instructor beings with the notes and scales, not arpeggios and pedaling nuance, because the foundational skills must be established first. Prospecting (or networking) is the foundational skill of selling.

It's a skill taken for granted during training and coaching because it is unnecessary in many sales roles. In retail sales for example, the buyer *comes* to the salesperson. Thus the emphasis on selling instruction begins with the processes of greeting customers and building rapport before conducting a discovery dialogue. In other words, the prospecting skill is less vital, although not irrelevant as proven by the story of Curtis and Tonto. In business-to-business selling, *prospecting* must occur or the rest of the process is moot. The salesperson must *find* the buyer first.

Sales economics is about the science of selling. Prospecting is the foundational skill. Armchair experts can have a lot of opinions about presentation skills, closing, handling conflict, and other more artistic skills of the process. The science we have established to this point demonstrates powerful links between prospecting, the value of an appointment, and deepening business-to-business relationships.

The appointment has already been established as a powerful KPI, specifically because it indicates sincere buying interest. If the buyer is unwilling to meet, the salesperson can presume interest is lacking. This is the reason the bid avoidance presentation is such a powerful behavioral sales asset. If the buyer willingly schedules a place, date, and time to meet, interest of some degree is proven and an opportunity has been established.

The appointment, however, is a single event during the course of a larger time frame. Anybody can have a moment of success. The proof of sales excellence is the ability to repeat success every day, week, and month. This is the power of calendar management.

Calendar Coaching in Action

Martin is a budding sales star who was among many that have endured the "ability and willingness" test of competence. He was given the usual instructions to prepare a perfect day and offered the same support, specifically to call if he struggled and needed assistance. The day I worked with him evolved into a typical day of sales adversity when the plans of Martin fell apart rapidly.

The first sales call was a scheduled visit with a highly unqualified buyer. His next planned stop was with a prospect who told him to call before arriving, then didn't answer the phone, and was not present when we arrived at his office. The next "appointment" was scheduled with a lead purchasing agent who would not be present and had delegated Martin to an assistant with no warning we would be arriving. After that mid-morning call, Martin apologetically told me he had nothing else lined up.

It wasn't a good day for Martin and obvious from his demeanor he was upset and slightly embarrassed, which is a good sign! If he weren't disappointed, it would have indicated he lacked motivation. I suggested that we start making cold calls and opened my iPhone. A Google search turned up several potential buyers in the area. For the remainder of the morning and three hours into the afternoon, we made cold calls. In between each cold call, the poor guy had to listen to me wax philosophically about sales, presentation skills, influence, and prospecting data. In other words, there was little idle chitchat and a lot of business theory being hurled at him.

Martin drove and followed my directions to the leads I found using Google maps. He endured my lectures and boldly walked into one office after another to make cold calls with me. He did it all while likely dealing with fear and concern about having a poorly constructed day with the hired consultant. At the conclusion of the day, using the sales call scorecard introduced in Chapter 12 (Figure 16.1), Martin scored seven points. He had six sales calls and the morning warm call. If we showed up at an office and were unable to speak with a contact, it didn't even count as a cold call. There were no meaningful dialogues, no leads, and no follow-up appointments. We could have fudged the scorecard a little by counting a few scribbled notes and getting a receptionist's name as extra points, but Bobby Jones wouldn't. As a day measured by the sales call points system, it was not a good showing for Martin.

Figure 16.1

As the afternoon waned, I suggested we head to his office. Of course the day wasn't yet over for Martin. We had at least an hour of "sales daylight" until the bell tolled at five o'clock. I suggested we make some phone calls. The "we" in this case was me. I would make cold calls with Martin until he could see what success looks like and recognize a model of performance quality to emulate. I asked him to open his computer and search for remodelers in the area and, without procrastination, made the first call.

"Good afternoon," I said to the receptionist. "I'm calling from Martin's Lumber Company to find out the best person to speak to about our products. May I ask your name?" Pause. "Shelley, I appreciate that. Sure, I'll hold." Pause. Martin couldn't hear, but I later told him the next voice on the line was curt, almost rude. "Rick calling form Martin's Lumber. Do you know us?" Quick pause. "We're a supplier of the types of products you use and we work with companies just like yours in the area. Would love to give you the names of several contractors we've helped. I'm calling to schedule a time to come in, learn a bit about your business, and see if we're a fit for you...or at least a candidate to be a backup supplier. What do you think?...Tomorrow...nine-thirty...What's your email? I'll send a confirmation...See you tomorrow!" I hung up the phone, a little surprised at the ease with which that happened on my first call.

Martin looked at me and said, "I wish that had been harder for you." I had to laugh and honestly assured him I got lucky, but that I also didn't get lucky. I confessed that I had gone through the same exercise with a salesman on the West Coast a month earlier and needed a dozen calls to get my first appointment. I assured him that my success rate is somewhere in between. The thing that was not lucky was the script. If you dissect it, you will see many phrases of tested behavioral sales economics that work.

We "can give you the names of several contractors we've helped" is a promise that someone else is saying good things about us, that it's not just bragging—i.e., the higher authority. Let's "see if we're a fit" assures the buyer we are sincere in our goal to help. We supply "the types of products you use" is a grabber to get attention to assure a credible supplier is available as an alternative. "What's your email? I'll send a confirmation" is the means to ensure the client is prepared and won't forget the meeting. The phrases are tested to work. It was ironic that the first call resulted in an appointment, but not lucky that we got it. I would have called five, seven, twelve, or whatever it took to get that first meeting. I owed it to my student. He had proven he was willing to do the work and I wanted to prove I was willing to do it with him.

It was Martin's turn to make phone calls while I watched him. His first call was clumsy and he asked for help on wording. We worked on some phrases and it took him only three more calls to schedule a meeting. He scheduled another meeting for the next day a few calls later.

It was just shy of five o'clock and Martin deserved to get a break from the pressure. We called it a day and discussed our plan for the next morning. Martin passed the "will he or won't he" test with flying colors. He stood up to the scrutiny of my observations, never made an excuse, endured the lectures, and in spite of the emotional exhaustion he must have been feeling, jumped on the phone with me to create a sales opportunity. Martin had *willingness*.

I think a lot of managers and coaches would have criticized the performance. They would *tell* the salesperson what was wrong and expect a better showing next time. Most managers are not willing to exercise the dull and tedious demonstration of the performance model necessary for success. A warrior leader jumps in to demonstrate skills on the field of battle. It's what Abe would do.

The next day Martin proved he *can* do the job. We had four appointments scheduled, the first with a remodeler who

Martin had met in his previous job. We left with a blueprint for a large home addition worth tens of thousands of dollars; more importantly it was a loyal buyer with whom we could expect to do many more projects; no next meeting was scheduled— seven points, a single call worth more than the entire previous day. That next appointment didn't result in an immediate lead, but the dialogue was solid—four points. Our next call was worth seven points, and the last appointment of the day yielded a tangible lead, a follow-up plan, and a scheduled future appointment on the calendar for a nine-point call. We squeezed in two cold calls, one of which yielded a contact who suggested Martin "call in a week or so," bringing his total point count for the day to twenty-nine points! Some salespeople go weeks without achieving that level of success and he did it in one day. The question now was whether he had the willingness without to do it again without the responsibility of performing in front of an audience, because we knew he had the ability. That is, would he do it on his own?

Predictable KRIs

A former client had hired a new sales rep and asked if I would do a ride along with him. Tracy is a twenty-year veteran and had been familiar with my work, so he agreed to let me join him. I believe in retrospect he might have merely been offering a courtesy he felt required as a new employee, but the day yielded good results.

We hit the road after building some personal rapport over a quick cup of coffee. Tracy took me on five sales calls, four scheduled appointments, and one warm call arising out of the third appointment. It was a clinic of sales excellence. His score for five calls was twenty-eight points. He displayed the skills, poise, and controlled competence one would expect but often doesn't see in a longtime sales veteran.

On the way back to the office, after having offered Tracy no coaching suggestions (nor being asked any), I asked him how he would rate his selling skills on a scale of ten. It felt to me that he expected me to suddenly take the opportunity find fault in his performance and tell him what he needed to work on. His answer was a strategic deflection and he cleverly said, "I don't know. Seven. Maybe eight." I chuckled and told him he was at least a nine, but added that I hardly know enough to discount the possibility he is a ten.

The manager and chief operating officer asked my opinion of him the next day and I gave it. I assured them that Tracy had the goods for success and his manager said, "I think so, too." Not to create controversy, I insisted there is no "think" about it. We can know. He's a star. He has ability and willingness. He probably didn't even want me to ride with him, but courteously permitted it. He was asked to put together the day of a star and, with no guidance or coaching, delivered…on the first try! That is a rarity.

Seven months later, he was the second-highest producer for three consecutive months and his sales were steadily increasing. Later dialogues with my client have reinforced the simple power of coaching observation. If you have a performer who can do it under the scrutiny of a watching eye, they *can* do it when you're not looking. You only need to verify over time if they will. If the salesperson can't do it while a coach is looking, there is either a deficiency of willingness or inability to address.

The Sum of the Parts

The rest of the calendar management story is not hard to figure. A single appointment repeated with success produces a solid day; a solid day leads to a productive month, which repeated produces a year of success. The calendar is a measurement of both quantity and quality. Having just one or the other is not enough.

As an example of performance quantity that failed the quality test, a former employer of mine required forty sales calls per week from each salesperson. The expectation was non-negotiable. I thought I was alone in my failure to succeed within the model until I attended a regional meeting with dozens of fellow salespeople. Few achieved the result because the model didn't account for administrative responsibilities, planning, and windshield time. Worse yet, those that satisfied the requirement of the forced metric, or came close, admittedly experienced low quality interactions.

They appeased the boss to create job security through forced activity, but failed to develop the professional skills that would lead to actual sales success through productivity. In short, the dictum was a theoretical construct not tested by actual performance and observation. It was devised to force transactional dependability by artificial means. The employer in this case was a company that had purchased the dealership where I had worked for years. The environment was one in which I felt uncomfortable, unproductive, and unappreciated. Like numerous other salespeople in this company with high turnover rates, I moved on.

At my next career stop, I was the test model for a sales program. I started by making lots of sales calls to our target audience, and "lots of sales calls" in this case included weeks of forty sales calls. Forty sales calls were certainly doable, but not sustainable. Over time, the interactions evolved and, although I was making fewer calls, between twenty and twenty-five, the quality of interactions improved. Less calls of quality are better than a large quantity of mediocre interactions.

Balance speaks to the power of KPI measurement of the sales call. One high-quality call is more valuable than a day of cold calls. Relying on transactional dependability with pop-in visits is not as powerful as meeting new associates and generating new leads on behalf of a reseller. The KPIs of the sales call produce predictive future results. Most importantly, a one-time success of a single day or a solid week of calendar success is hardly as powerful as a consistent campaign of calendar management.

Balance speaks to the power of calendar evolution. Early in the salesperson's career or tenure with an employer, more calls are possible because they emphasize prospecting and start-up growth. As the market and performer matures, the tenor of sales calls progresses. The percentage of sales calls to prospects, which is high in the beginning, starts to shift. More sales interactions occur with existing customers in need of service support and opportunities to earn ongoing transactions. The career evolves from transactional launch to transactional sustainability.

Eventually the sales model I had developed and piloted enabled me to earn the role as the national sales director for a newly formed department. Having been in the field for over a decade, my reporting structure was intentionally designed to produce more success for performers and require minimal documentation. In short, the salespeople on my staff provided two reports.

The first was a weekly summary report of activity. The objective was to eliminate subjectivity and creative writing embellishments of performance. Instead, sales representatives were expected to provide a summary for the number of calls per week; the relative value of the customer or prospect account rated by category—A, B, or C; and the "temperature" by which the meetings were scheduled—appointment, warm call, or cold call. The results were revealing.

Three of my sale reps consistently packed more meetings into the week. A few couldn't stand up to the scrutiny of performance standards and moved on. A few were somewhere in between. I've been asked many times how I could know whether their reports were truthful or counterfeit and the answer is inspection.

It's an old cliché to inspect what you expect. The power of observation, if you are a manager, is to perform a day of coaching in the field with the expectation of *the perfect day*. A salesperson who delivers a report that portrays twenty-six sales calls with nine grade-A accounts and includes the claim to have made eleven appointments ought to be able to prove it by producing a day congruous with the report when the manager is watching.

The power is in the measurement and periodic inspection and, when necessary, field coaching. The KPIs of the sales call have established a newly created scale of performance. The call itself is a single component of the larger picture of successful calendar management. A series of single calls add up to a day; five days add up to a week; weeks add up to months, and eventually one-year campaigns.

The weekly report was one of the two vital measurements of performance excellence. The other was the value of prospecting leads generated, the ultimate source of results, and the subject for the next chapter.

17

Predictable Sales Results

Rearview Mirror Management

Try driving ahead while staring into your rearview mirror and see how long you can last on your journey. Early in the journey of sales economics discovery, you read about organizations that fall short of sales objectives and earnings reports because they lack a game plan on offense. A lot of experts know *what* is supposed to happen, but not *how*.

As a result, sales plans are measured in the rearview mirror. Instead of translating goals into KPIs that matter, long-term outcomes are established and then broken down into intermediate outcomes. In the case of sales results, these outcomes are usually broken down into monthly sales KRIs (key results indicators), although still measured after the fact.

You wouldn't drive a car by staring in the rearview mirror, and
you shouldn't drive your sales plans by looking in the past either.

The "Rearview Mirror" Management
of Future Sales Goals

This year's goal	=	<u>$1,200,000</u>
January	=	72,000
February	=	89,000
March	=	61,000
April	=	106,000
May	=	91,000
June	=	<u>62,000</u>
YTD	=	$481,000

Figure 17.1: After the annual sales goal is established, performance is
tracked on a periodic basis. If the desired results are achieved, the performer
is thought to be executing well. If not, then pressure is applied with the hope
that the salesperson knows how to fix the problem. This results in the circular
conversation of blame illustrated earlier in the book. The manager expects the
salesperson to have a solution or simply work harder while the salesperson
seeks guidance to relieve the pressure.

Figure 17.1 illustrates a typical review of sales progress
over a six-month period for a performer assigned the goal of
$1,200,000 in annual sales. Each month the KRI of monthly
sales is reviewed relative to the annual goal. In this illustration,
the monthly KRI for the salesperson is $100,000. Ignoring for
the moment how the long-term sales goal was established, it's
clear from this illustration that the salesperson is falling short
of the objective.

Ask almost any veteran salesperson and they will agree
that, at some point in their career, they were faced with the

daunting task of achieving a goal they felt was out of reach. A long-term sales goal was set, possibly without the salesperson's input, and tracked as the primary criterion of sales success. This methodology, besides being ineffective, creates anxiety that makes it difficult for salespeople to perform at optimum levels. More importantly, the rearview mirror management approach provides no KPIs upon which the salesperson or organization can rely.

Start with Transactional Dependability

The sales economics concept of transactional dependability, which has already been defined as the measurement of transactional customer retention, provides an ideal starting point to establish future goals. Transactional dependability is one of the easiest measurements to make while providing clarity for future sales planning.

Abe Isaacson sat with his pupil, Noah, and began planning the sales campaign for an upcoming year. Noah's goal had been established by executives in the organization to reach $3,000,000. After receiving his budget, Noah panicked.

"I grew my territory by ten percent last year," said Noah. "Now you're asking me to increase fifteen percent this year from $2,600,000 to $3,000,000. That seems like a big jump."

Abe saw no value in telling Noah there was truth to his argument. Like Noah, Abe had been handed budgets from executives for sales requirements based on calculations to maximize return on capital investment. Instead of lamenting the situation, Abe had a plan and insights to offer his student.

"The good news is that a lot of your work has already been done for you," Abe said. "You can depend on your existing widget customers. In fact, we can assign a fairly definite value to that number."

"I'd like to think that sales from my existing customer base will increase and that I won't have to find as much new business," Noah said hopefully.

"It's a bad idea to think that way," Abe said. Then he opened his computer to show Noah a history of his sales over the previous three years. "I did some analysis. All the information we need to calculate the level of customer retention is right here in the computer. The records show that two years ago you retained most of your business from the previous year, eighty-three percent to be exact. Last year, you actually did a little better by retaining eighty-eight percent. It's really interesting to note that some of your customers dropped off, possibly from neglect or perhaps just because they went out of business.

"So we should figure that you will retain around eighty-five percent of your business from the previous year heading into next year. We should also review your accounts individually to make sure that we lose as few as possible. This can be done with phone calls, emails, and personal visits. Make sense?"

Noah stared at the computer screen and, although he wasn't feeling particularly confident, at least he had some facts to work with. He agreed that it made perfect mathematical sense, but added, "That still means I need to find a lot more business while still replacing a lot of lost business."

"Oh good!" Abe said with a laugh. "Then you get it! You don't need $400,000 in new business. It's more like $800,000. Piece of cake!" He drew numbers on paper to help his pupil see.

Noah's Contract

Sales Goal =	$3,000,000
(Previous Year = $2,600,000)	
(Retention Rate = 85%)	
Retained Sales =	$2,200,000
New Sales =	$ 800,000

Figure 17.2: The upcoming goal of $3,000,000 is poorly planned by rearview mirror management of $250,000 per month. A better plan establishes sales retention of $2,200,000 of previous year $2,600,000 based on a rate of 85% *transactional dependability*. The retained sales $2,200,000 subtracted from the upcoming goal of $3,000,000 calculates to $800,000 of needed sales growth.

Noah wanted to laugh, but was still feeling anxiety. "The way I figure it," he said, "is that I need to average $250,000 in sales per month to succeed. Right?"

Abe agreed that that was one way to look at it, but added, "I wouldn't think that way because it tells you how many points you need to put on the board, but not how to get there. There is a better way. Would you like to know?"

Intergalactic Laws of Math

"I guess," said Noah. He was feeling pretty anxious, particularly because he saw the words at the top of Abe's notepad and asked, "Why did you write 'Noah's Contract'?"

"Well," Abe said thoughtfully. "I can't do it for you. Our organization is asking you to reach the goal, but can't hit it for you. So I guess there are a few ways to look at it. To me the best way is to figure the company we work for is our customer. Let's give our customer the best possible service we can offer.

It's all we can do. Then, to make a personal game out of it, why not just make a contract with yourself? If you agree to the contract, you'll be off and running. If not, well…then I guess there is Plan B."

"What's Plan B?" Noah asked without hesitation.

Abe laughed. "How about you and I start with Plan A and we'll work from there?"

He had never heard the concept of high or low transactional dependability, but Abe was on to something. He knew that he could instill confidence in his performer by converting the daunting task of large, long-term results into bite-size units of accomplishment. He leaned back in his chair to explain some logic that he believed was incontrovertible.

"Think about this," Abe said thoughtfully. "Your rate of customer retention is similar to other salespeople in the organization and, by my estimation, probably pretty typical of our industry in this market. Would you agree?"

Noah's eyes squinted as he considered the truth of Abe's statement and finally conceded with a nod, "Yeah. I *would* agree with that. It makes sense, but why would it matter?"

"I'll tell you exactly why! If the rate of customer retention in the market is eighty-five percent, then it tells us that the average rate at which we take business from our customers must be fifteen percent," Abe concluded.

Noah started running the calculations in his mind and, if Abe were correct, it meant the consequent implications of prospecting were very high. Noah doubted Abe's conclusion and felt that he probably had a much higher closing ratio, or at least wanted to think so.

"No," said Abe. "There is no doubt about it. It is as true as the intergalactic law of mathematics. If the average rate of customer retention is eighty-five percent anywhere in the universe, the average rate at which a competitor takes the business away is, by definition, fifteen percent. I'll concede that some salespeople will outperform others by slight percentages. In fact, Noah, you're very good at sales and influence. Your calendar management is superior. Your prospecting energy is on target. It would not surprise me if you close at a slightly better ratio than the market average.

"But even if you do, it's probably a safer bet to plan conservatively and hope to outperform the market average. So, if you need $800,000 in new business, then you need to be *prospecting* approximately $450,000 per month." Abe emphasized the word prospecting to clarify to his student that he shouldn't worry about the KRI, but instead focus on the KPI under his control.

Noah couldn't decide whether he really wanted to doubt the math or simply avoid the cosmic truth. He wasn't alone. Most salespeople prefer to ignore the obvious truth of mathematic prospecting calculations, if they even have an understanding of them at all. It's like the head coach that ignores the game plan because he doesn't understand the game. If you understand the MaSE game of goal achievement, prospecting goals make perfect sense.

Calculate Prospecting Necessity

Noah was having a hard time following Abe's logic and asked how he came up with his cockamamie numbers. Abe laughed and wrote more on a separate piece of paper. He scribbled the math and explained the logic to his young apprentice. The needed sales growth had been established by subtracting the value of retained sales—i.e., transactional dependability— from the future goal. He established a sales growth goal (G) based on that math and presumed logically that, if the market stayed relatively flat, the closing ratio (c) would be the inverse of rate for transactional dependability to establish a prospecting objective (P).

Setting the Prospecting Goal

If, P x c = G
Then, (P x c)/c = G/c
$$P = G/c$$

Where: G = Growth Goal; c = Closing Ratio;
P = Prospecting Necessity to Achieve KRIs

Figure 17.3: Of three variables for controlled sales growth, only prospecting is under the control of the performer, even if closing ratios might be slightly higher than the market average for an individual. By definition, the average closing ratio for new business must be the inverse of customer retention in a given market, presuming flat sales for the entire market. Therefore, if prospecting volume (P) multiplied by the closing ratio (c) equals sales growth (G), then a definitive prospecting goal for success equals G/c.

Noah couldn't decide whether he really wanted to doubt the math or simply avoid the cosmic truth of his prospecting necessity (P), which is the prospecting requirement needed to achieve the sales growth goal. Figure 17.3 provides the mathematical calculation of prospecting necessity that follows from indisputable mathematics. After determining growth goal (G) to achieve a future sales goal, the rest of the process is algebraic.

P x c = G is a certainty in a historical context. After the fact, a salesperson could measure these variables, although it would be too late. The goal is to plan for future predictability. If P x c = G is a "historic" measurement of past performance. The real goal is to determine what future performance is necessary.

Of the three variables in the equation, contrary to instinct, the only one under the control of the performer is *prospecting* (P). Most salespeople would like to believe they can increase closing ratios to dramatically outperform the market but, as Abe has proven, closing ratios are a market average that is indisputable. Simple algebra enables us to isolate the value of P by dividing both sides of the equation by closing ratio (c). Thus, (P x c)/c = G/c or P = G/c. Thus it is proven (QED). Prospecting necessity is defined as the growth goal (G) (i.e., transactional necessity) divided by a predictable closing ratio (calculated by example in Figure 17.3).

Noah watched silently as Abe diligently went into a deep thinking mode and scribbled numbers and equations on his notepad (Figure 17.4). Abe considered the logic of his exercise and looked up at Noah with words on the tip of his tongue before deciding to withhold the complicated contingencies flowing through his mind. Abe considered several flaws in his plan.

Noah's Contract

Sales Goal =	**$3,000,000**
(Previous Year = $2,600,000)	
(Retention Rate = 85%)	
Retained Sales =	**<u>$2,200,000</u>**
New Sales =	**$ 800,000**

If, $\left\{ \begin{array}{l} P = G/c \\ P = \$800{,}000 / 15\% \\ P = \$5{,}333{,}333 \end{array} \right\}$ then... $\left\{ \begin{array}{l} P^A = \$5{,}333{,}333 \\ P^M = \$\ \ 450{,}000 \\ P^W = \$\ \ 100{,}000 \end{array} \right\}$

Figure 17.4: The power to achieve any goal is contingent on establishing performance benchmarks within the control of the performer. In this case, the annual sales goal of $3,000,000 has been converted to a annual prospecting goal (P^A), a monthly objective (P^M), and a weekly one (P^W). The methodology won't guarantee success if the prospecting values are not feasible, but at least converts daunting long-term goals into visible short-term action plans.

The first and most obvious was that the market itself could rise. If so, that meant that retained sales might grow with it…or sink with it if the market falls. He also considered the complexities of measuring prospecting values. He considered the possibility that sales of new products to existing customers might be a source of sales growth and, moreover, might close at better rates than average. He recognized that the numbers he came up with were rounded up or down to create a vision of simplicity for the performer rather than exact, theoretical numbers. Other small flaws of logic enter his mind, each of which he dismissed as a matter of practicality.

Cover your assignment. Outhit your man. Commit less turnovers. *Zip-Whoosh!* Simple is better he concluded as the theory of a fourteenth-century English theologian named

William of Ockham popped into his head. The theory became known as Occam's razor. He asserted that any plan had lower chances for success in inverse proportion to the increase in variables. For every variable he might include, Abe rationalized, new complications arose that were not germane to the exercise.

The vision of his goal-setting formula was clear and could be executed without adding unnecessary mathematics, at least for the moment. All the additional contingencies and variables would make it difficult for a salesperson to focus on the simple task at hand. Prospect to a singular value. Success, Abe concluded, could be that simple. He turned the paper to Noah (Figure 17.4) and slid it forward. He explained the simplicity of his mathematics and then drew a circle around the key statistic that Abe believed mattered most.

"I think you've got this," Abe said to Noah. "At least you have a plan. Instead of constantly worrying about the sales results, which are not under your control, here is a chance to focus on the one thing you can control. That is your ability to prospect and network. What do you think?"

Noah studied the paper as questions flowed through his mind. He still doubted the closing ratios and felt he might do better, but accepted Abe's assertion about market averages because it made sense. He wondered if there were enough opportunities in the market to prospect at that level. Finally he asked, "If my average sale is only $20,000 or so, how can I find $450,000 per month?"

Abe quickly said, "It's not about the average sale; it's about the average opportunity. There is a big difference."

Noah looked puzzled and asked what difference there could be.

Abe said, "Let's say you talk to your typical customer, someone who is likely to purchase your materials repeatedly over the course of year. In your case, it's a contractor who is capable of buying $20,000 of widgets…only instead of once, he buys a shipment eight times per year. You have a few customers like that, yes?"

Noah pondered his mentor's words and nodded.

"Good. So that is not a $20,000 opportunity really, is it?"

Noah got it immediately. "No," he said. "I see. It's a $160,000 opportunity."

"How common are those types of leads in your territory?" Abe asked.

Noah confessed that there were a lot of them before volunteering, "I guess I would only need about three of those per month to hit my prospecting goal, but I probably won't make sales with them all."

Abe chuckled and said, "You've just made my point. You don't have to make a sale to all of them. In fact, you only need to close five of those in a year! Five times $160,000 equals $800,000. Can you do that?"

Noah looked up with honest surprise and stifled his delight. It was almost embarrassing to him to consider how simple the game plan was. "Am I supposed to sign the contract?" he asked sincerely.

"For whom?" Abe asked.

"You…I guess. I don't know. Is that what you're asking me to do? Sign the contract?"

Abe smiled and said, "No. It's your contract. It's for you. If you think it will work, which I believe it will, then commit yourself to it. Negotiate with yourself if you must. Decide for yourself. But, once you've decided, then have the courage to fulfill the commitment to yourself. Deal?"

Noah took the paper, looked at Abe, and said, "Deal."

Abe asked his pupil, "Did I ever tell you the story of Bobby Jones assessing himself a one stroke penalty?"

Noah smiled and said, "Yep. More than once."

Abe laughed at himself and let the dialogue fade. It was clear he had settled a nervous student by reducing a seemingly unattainable goal to a very simple performance plan.

The KPIs of Long-Term Success

If you want to lose weight, you determine what foods you will eat and how many calories you will budget. You factor in the amount of exercise and calories you will burn. Then you start the plan and stick with it. The challenges of long-term sales prospecting measurement include defining lead quality, assessing the value of leads, and tracking.

Lead quality is a process that requires the objective evaluation of subjectivity. Earlier, when Abe and Noah had been analyzing the quality of a sales call, Abe pointed out that the interest from the customer without a request for pricing was a powerful indicator. A request for pricing is not necessarily an indicator of sincere interest, which is the reason the bid avoidance presentation is a powerful exercise in lead qualification. The objective judgment of lead quality is based on the subjective observation of dialogue. If a potential buyer expresses sincere interest in a dialogue regarding a specific product, then the salesperson can presume the lead is valid and worth including in the tracking of prospecting necessity.

In short, it is not enough to *want* the business to count it as a viable lead. The buyer has to express interest.

The KPIs of Annual Sales Achievement

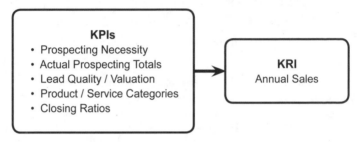

Figure 17.5: The KPIs of sales achievement include numerous calculations under the control of the performer. Prospecting necessity is the calculation to be broken down into annual, monthly, and even weekly performance objectives. The key to success is measuring actual prospecting totals against necessity. This includes valuation of leads, isolating specific opportunities, and eventually establishing actual closing ratios of performance.

Lead valuation is a challenge that creates a struggle for many salespeople. As a salesman of windows, I found many buyers interested in sincere product dialogues without a price being requested, which we have already established as a good sign. Let's suppose I am talking to a builder who typically produces between six and eight homes per year. Any salesperson with moderate experience ought to be able to guess the value of a purchase based on the size of the home. In this case, the builder is using a vinyl window on a home that is approximately 1,800 square feet. The safe calculation is to say the builder will use 12 windows valued at $200 each. Rather than estimate liberally, a conservative estimate of 6 houses allows me, as the window salesman, to presume the lead is worth 6 (houses) x 12 (windows) x $200 = $14,400.

The estimate is not perfect, but it's close enough. Certainly the best guess calculation of lead value is better than not tracking the lead at all. In business-to-business sales, the value of a lead should align with the presumptive future commitment. This means that a lead to a repeat purchaser should not be measured in terms of a single transaction, but in the series of them over the course of a year. The annual value of a lead for repeat purchases aligns with the annual prospecting objective.

In cases where repeat purchase commitments should not be expected, then a one-time value should be assessed. This would be true in a setting for commercial construction. For example, a supplier of commercial roofing products might engage in dialogue with a general contractor for a large factory. The contractor is not likely to be capable of estimating annual purchases and, moreover, typically doesn't provide the loyalty of a residential builder. Therefore this is a lead that should be assessed in terms of a one-time value.

Lead specificity means defining the lead in product (or service) specific terms. For example, the salesperson selling building materials that include lumber, roofing, windows, flooring, kitchens, and a multitude of other products must determine when authentic interest has been established in a product, one at a time. A salesperson naturally tries to their company as a "one-stop shop" with the hope that the buyer will make the quantum leap to buy all products from a single source.

The reality is that salespeople think in terms of selling the whole package while buyers seek specialists by category. The key to prospecting measurement success for any salesperson means defining prospecting opportunities one product and service at a time. In other words, it isn't enough for a salesperson to say, "I'm just going to try to get all their business." This is a fine dream, but not a quality calculation. The salesperson would do better to learn that a client or prospect is struggling with one or two specific products and target those as opportunities. Thus, instead of tracking a client falsely as a prospecting opportunity for "all services," it would be better for the salesperson to isolate the two specific opportunities of client interest. Specificity matters.

Trust the percentages. Customer relationship management (CRM) software notoriously creates something I call a *false funnel of escalating percentages.* One product on the market calculates the closing ratio on a new sale at 10% after the *initial communication.* The ratio rises to 25% after *needs assessment,* then jumps to 40% after the *presentation.* The next stage is *proposal,* which raises closing ratios to 65%; and finally *commitment to buy,* which puts closing ratios at 80%. These are handy pieces of data imported by a computer programmer that have no bearing on reality. Closing ratios should be calculated using estimations based in reality until actual data are available.

In Noah's case, the 15% closing ratio is a good estimate to start. For all business-to-business salespeople, the inverse ratio of transactional dependability is a solid closing ratio to employ at the start of the journey. For business-to-consumer salespeople—e.g., the mattress or car salesperson—the best ratio to use is the actual ratio that can be measured in the short term.

The longer the sales cycle, the more difficult it will be to establish an actual closing ratio. For example, a mattress salesperson can calculate an actual closing ratio by reviewing a single month and count on reasonable accuracy. Conversely, the typical sales cycle for a lumber salesperson is between three and twelve months. The best way to accurately calculate a closing ratio for the lumber salesperson is to review the past year of leads and actual closing values, which presents a problem.

If the salesperson has to wait a year to generate an actual closing ratio, productivity is lost for that period. Therefore, instead of waiting a year to create an actual closing ratio, it is best to estimate one using the best means available.

The Contract of Your Career

Abe wrote a "contract" for Noah to establish with himself. The macrosales economics of goal setting and achievement can be established with a high degree of certainty. The process is simple, albeit not easy. There is subjectivity in the analysis of lead quality and value that improves over time. Closing ratios are uncertain as the beginning of a campaign. Market conditions will have an effect on rates of account attrition and growth.

The real power in Abe's approach with his student is the factual basis of the dialogue. An annual goal that is delegated to the salesperson can create anxiety and disbelief. Abe provided a methodology for Noah to break down the goal into management performance segments—KPIs that matter and are under the full control of the performer.

Abe noted the complications and even some pitfalls of the process, but came to one undeniable truth. It's better to have a simple plan that can be adjusted later than no plan at all. *Zip-Whoosh!*

18

Creating Sales Advocacy

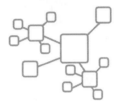

Teach Others to Tell Your Story

In the hustle and bustle of downtown Las Vegas sits Hugo's Cellar, a calm haven on the lower level of the Four Queens Casino. It is one of the great old-school steak houses in the country and, if you are inclined to buy a bottle of wine while dining, John the sommelier is your man. The experience he offers is one of numerous highlights my friends and I anticipate during our annual meal at Hugo's Cellar.

Expect John to approach your table with a small metal tasting cup hanging from a chain around his neck, which he uses to sample each bottle before pouring it for his guests. He starts a lively conversation to put his customers at ease before efficiently shifting to the business of wine selection. Rest assured he will take an order for the bottle you choose, but you'd be wiser to let him make a recommendation.

Without fail, John suggests excellent wines always within a few dollars of the price range requested. He provides a wonderful sense of humor, decorum, and a deep knowledge of wine enhanced by his direct connections with visiting vintners and tours of their wineries. The wines he recommends consistently come with a reference to the conversation he had with a winery representative or often the owner of the winery. John is a consummate professional and, in this role, the classic example of transactional sales advocacy.

Transactional advocacy was already defined earlier to *occur when a supplier impacts the behaviors of individual resellers to create brand or product advocacy that increases transactional dependability.* The smart winery salespeople know to influence John because he, in turn, will influence the end buyer. John has complete credibility and possesses something referred to earlier as the respect of the *higher authority.* John provides the credibility the winery itself cannot.

I have referred a few times to the *higher authority,* which is *an expert that the buyer values as an objective arbiter of value.* The higher authority is seen as the unbiased advisor. If the manufacturer's sales rep for a product tells you his brand is the best, it's hardly objective advice. If the retail salesperson, having numerous brands from which to choose, provides the same advice, it is highly credible.

If the winery had written the most flowering and detailed recommendation for its wine, it would have been a helpful buying hint taken with a healthy degree of skepticism. Moreover, a vintner could spend hours regaling the restaurant owner and manager about the glory of their wine, but won't stand a chance of selling my mates and me a bottle until they get John's stamp of approval. He is a higher authority and the professional *advocate* with direct access to the final buyers in the supply chain.

If there is a better way to influence potential buyers by telling your story, it is by getting someone else to tell it for you. Expensive red wine is a product where a higher authority wields an especially strong influence, for good reason. There are thousands of wines to choose from and it is impossible for a casual diner to truly know them all. Therefore the advocate wields credible influence to be leveraged.

Advocates are powerful influencers for millions of sales decisions every day. You buy the brand of heater and air-conditioning unit based on the advocacy of an impartial arbiter, specifically the installer who can choose from numerous products and knows which works best based on the years of experience that a consumer cannot possibly obtain. My remodeling contractor, Randy, *told* my wife which plumbing fixtures were best and she shopped for *only* one brand, the one an impartial advocate had recommended. Torsten, one of the top bike mechanics in the Chicago area and a salesperson for the Highland Park Trek Bicycle Store, *told* me not only the specific bicycle model, but every accessory to be included; I listened and bought exactly what he recommended.

It's easy to ignore the frontline soldiers on the way to the corporate office because the traditional "decision-maker" is the primary, and important, selector of the brands to carry in the store…but only the first stage of the sale. The sale to a reseller occurs on two levels, the first being the *commitment* offered by the executive decision-maker to determine which brands will be carried in the store. The second is to create *advocacy*, after the commitment is earned, from salespeople who promote to the next level in the supply chain such as retail knife salespeople, sommeliers, heating and air-conditioning installers, plumbers, bike mechanics, and other direct influencers of transactional decisions.

Store managers influence the final sale minimally; salespeople reselling the product to the next level in the supply chain influence the sale greatly. And they do it within the confines of daily pressure that create a powerful illustration of behavioral sales economic decisions at work.

Behavioral Resale Economics

It's the middle of the day for a counter sales clerk earning an hourly wage at the lumberyard. The phone is ringing and tasks are piling up. Professional homebuilders and product installers are pulling up in pickup trucks to get orders filled. Paperwork is being processed for contractors *not* picking up goods but instead relying on accurate and timely deliveries. Internal customers—i.e., salespeople, managers, and other coworkers—are making demands by way of text messages and phone calls while the sales clerk is trying to cope with rising administrative duties. Two manufacturer sales representatives, with nothing better to do than drive a sales route, pop in to chat with the clerk who is glancing at the clock in hopes of getting back on task. The manager of the location drops a set of blueprints on the desk of the clerk and asks for a pricing proposal to be completed by the end of the day. In short, there is a lot of pressure and little time for breaks.

The moment of advocacy arrives when a builder walks in with a blueprint and requests pricing on stair parts for a new home. The brand is not as important to the builder as the accuracy and timeliness of delivery. Stair parts are tricky because the order requires expertise. If the order is wrong, the builder will be delayed on the project and the lumberyard might have to accept a costly return on goods that cannot easily be resold. Most importantly, a multitasking employee with no financial incentive to choose one product over another is about to make a decision. The sales clerk has three different manufacturers as available suppliers. Which one is chosen?

Polling of my customers has consistently proven that the sales clerk makes a product selection in a matter of seconds based on the level of comfort with a specific brand. The criteria for the decision include familiarity with ordering procedures; comfort with the unique product brand terminology; access to a product representative; experience ordering the product without problems; and, perhaps most significantly, staying out of trouble.

The "best" choice in the mind of the sales clerk is not a matter of product feature comparisons. The clerk is like every other advocate and chooses the product based on personal bias. It's not that the sales clerk would promote a product that is inferior to other choices. In fact, it is just the opposite; sales clerks choose the products they believe are best, which for them has a lot to do with minimizing risks for their clients and avoiding problems with their employer. It's not only product quality that matters; it's getting the job done in the midst of a ridiculously hectic day.

Face it: there are a lot of high-quality products on the market. The sales clerk is not making a mistake by recommending any one of three choices for stair parts. Therefore, the manufacturer sales rep for the brand must recognize the truth of behavioral sales economic decisions. The sales clerks drive transactions and the best way to enhance transactional dependability is to build a team of sales advocates that, in the split second of decision-making, make the choice to promote the manufacturer's specific product.

This flies in the face of common sales practices of manufacturer sales reps who routinely delegate details of ordering and administrative fulfillment to representatives at the home office. Manufacturer sales reps too often see themselves as "pitch experts" and emphasize the value of their product's features and benefits. It's a presentation process learned at the factory and drilled into reps as a means of transferring the same knowledge to resellers. It's not *wrong*; it's just not *enough* to create brand loyalty. The key to success is *establishing confident competence in the product line.*

Pursuing Advocacy

The genesis of advocacy measurement evolved during an exciting debate at a client sales meeting with a stair parts company. A new pricing policy was being rolled out as the means to stabilize margins that consequently removed negotiation authority from the hands of salespeople. My role as the dialogue facilitator was to help salespeople see value in the new pricing structure.

One veteran sales representative, Charley, adamantly asserted the new program would not work in his market. He assured his executives that sales will be lost if he did not retain authority to negotiate for his clientele. It was a good opportunity to engage the Socratic questioning process.

Socrates was known for his abilities to direct people to the right conclusion, not with persuasive statements, but instead with leading questions.

The meeting had been derailed by this disagreeable veteran salesperson. His position as the self-appointed spokesperson of logic would hopefully enable a meaningful dialogue that could lead the sales team to a consensus even if Charley never agreed with it. So I asked him, "You believe it's possible to adequately have the information necessary to negotiate every deal in your market?"

"I do," Charley said with justifiable defense to his capabilities as a sales and negotiation expert. He actually was a high margin producer and, if all salespeople in the company had been as successful as he, a new pricing structure might not have been necessary. Unfortunately for Charley, the company chose to standardize pricing across the board rather than selectively allow some salespeople negotiation authority.

"So, the negotiation process looks like this, yes?" I took the flip chart in the room and drew the supply chain flow as I understood it for my client. The drawing you see in Figure 18.1 illustrates the simplicity of a single sale through the channel.

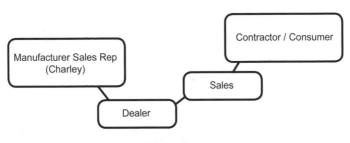

Figure 18.1

"You promote to a dealer where the salesman is involved with a contractor or consumer with whom a sale won't be made unless you are able to help negotiate the final price. Correct?"

Charley said, "That is how it works. Some sales they make on their own. But sometimes they need my help."

As a lesson in the Socratic method, know that you should have your objectives clear before the questions start. In this case, two points need to be made. First, it is very doubtful that any manufacturer sales rep is negotiating on behalf of the customer to *raise* prices. Second, a salesperson operating in a two-state territory with three major metropolitan markets and numerous other secondary markets is unlikely to have the proper and complete information necessary to justify pricing discretion in every transaction of the hundreds that would occur in a year. These are the two points I set out to prove.

"Right now your dealers have standardized pricing levels, correct?" I asked, "at least as starting points."

Charley said that was exactly how it worked.

It is a hard and fast rule in group meetings (at least for me) that a speaker or facilitator should avoid embarrassing an attendee at all costs. There is no equity in it for the presenter or the audience. Thus, I delicately asked, "Charley, your clients have parts and pricing lists. So…if they call, I can only assume it's to seek a discount, yes? It feels doubtful that any reseller is calling you or the home office to ask for a price *increase*."

Fortunately Charley is not only a veteran, but a thick-skinned one at that, who laughed with the group and said, "If that ever happens, I'll let you know!"

I laughed with him and assured him I want to hear about *that* story, because it would be a first! "Bottom line," I said, "is that you need to have the ability to *reduce* pricing when you feel it's appropriate, yes?"

He agreed and then I asked, "So how do you know?"

Charley pointed to my drawing (Figure 18.1) and said that he gets involved. He asks questions to get a sense of the competition and where they are pricing. He admitted that he doesn't always get to see the competitors' pricing, but "trusts the dealer." This answer created a murmur of doubt in the room because it inferred Charley didn't have all the adequate information, might be biased in his judgments, and was likely leaving valuable profits on the table. As a means to sincerely understand the situation I asked, "So the dealer is deciding between two suppliers and we aren't sure if they are offering the same flexibility you are seeking, correct?"

I got a better answer than expected when Charley said, "Oh. The dealer is selling my product. He's committed. The problem is the other dealer, my customer's competitor, is lowballing."

At that moment I suggested the hypothetical reasons his customer would be asking for a reduced price. "Or the salesman for the dealer is misinformed," I suggested, "or not a confident salesperson…or possibly even just testing the waters to get a lower price as a way to increase the dealer margins for a sale that might be made anyway. All of those are possibilities, but we really don't know. Would you agree with that, Charley?"

He agreed those were possibilities, but that he vets them each time, to which I asserted, "My belief is that *any* sales rep in your position can't possibly have the required information at hand to adequately negotiate *all* the deals happening in your market."

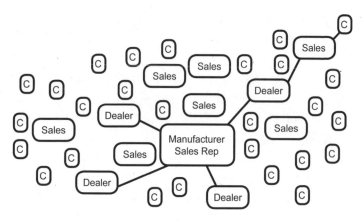

Figure 18.2

I started to draw more pictures, as economists are prone to do, to illustrate a powerful point. More questions were asked of Charley and the room at large. We concluded that the average salesperson in the room had between ten and fifteen highly active dealers in their markets. Of those dealers, some had one or two salespeople and others might have more than a dozen.

I started drawing boxes, letters, and words until it illustrated a chaotic market with hundreds of moving parts and people as depicted in Figure 18.2, where C represents professional contractors and consumers. It illustrated that a sales representative could be working in a market of several dozen potential sales advocates, each of whom influences the purchases for dozens of clients. In short, the stair parts manufacturer representative might have hundreds or even thousands of annual buyers one or two steps removed on the supply chain.

The room agreed that *any* salesperson, in this chaotic environment, would have a difficult time effectively managing dozens of negotiations each month from a level two or three times removed from the final buyer. Ergo, the best solution to create influence and more sales transactions is not to negotiate the pricing on the hundreds of sales per year, but instead create more promotional energy with sales advocates possessing higher authority with buyers.

This is not an illustration limited to the manufacturer, of course. Sales advocacy works anywhere in the supply chain when a salesperson can influence the unbiased authority of a salesperson one step closer to the final decision-maker. This is a powerful key to success in the age of Yelp and Google reviews. The things you say about you and your services are not nearly as important as the things other people say. Case studies and testimonials are your credibility currency.

"It's possible, just possible," I concluded to the group, "that we might do well with standardized pricing and still get the sale without concessions. It feels like our best opportunity at sales growth is not to constantly negotiate, but instead to build a team of sales advocates who promote for us assertively, at fair and established price levels, when we are not looking. Agreed?"

The Socratic exchange worked and the group agreed. The consensus was enhanced by a dialogue about fractals.

Fractal Selling

Fractals are geometric patterns that repeat at progressively smaller scales. They are seen throughout nature in plants, mollusks, galaxies, snowflakes, and other phenomenon. In the process of building advocacy, the concept of fractals can be a powerful visual asset for success. The usual practice for salespeople at the start of a supply chain, as already proven, is to emphasize contact with leading decision-makers at client offices. This is an excellent beginning and an essential aspect of building brand commitment.

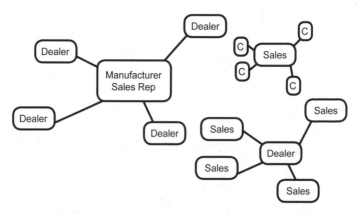

Figure 18.3

The advocacy model requires the salesperson to intentionally develop more fractals. As you look at Figure 18.3, you see the original model of success where the salesperson calls on the dealers, but also a repeating model of sales success. The next fractal occurs by building advocacy with salespeople within the dealer and ultimately repeats itself when individual salespeople become advocates who enthusiastically promote to the audience at the next level in the supply chain.

The end result is a system of sales fractals (Figure 18.4) that creates residual returns on time invested in selling—i.e., transactional dependability.

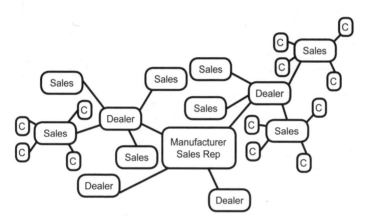

Figure 18.4

One salesperson at the stair parts meeting volunteered that he couldn't rationalize the requests for dealer discounts and felt caught in the middle of the customer and his employer. He believed the fractal model of advocacy was the answer to his problem. "If I can't negotiate, then the buyer knows they are receiving the best possible price; it's possible *more* confidence is created in the price structure." Not that the new price structuring was up for negotiation, but confidence in the program was key to success for the organization. The fact that a new level of comfort was being created improved chances for a seamless transition to standardized pricing.

"So, if I'm not negotiating to help close deals, then what *am* I doing to grow my business?" one salesman asked.

"You're going to measure advocacy," I said with excitement. "It's a measurement of your territory completely under your control that produces lasting results."

"Advocacy?" he asked.

"Yep," I said. "Here is how it works."

Competent Confidence

The sales team conceded that stair parts don't engender a high degree of brand loyalty until the reseller has had a positive experience with the brand. Therefore, the mission for each manufacturer rep was to create *confident competence* to order and promote the product.

Start with the premise that human beings resist change in direct proportion to their age and the complexity of their environment. In the case of the stair parts company, the complexity of the sales environment was so high that we could discount age as a factor. The people to whom the manufacturer promoted were dealing with multiple product categories, each with multiple brands, while managing audiences of different levels of expertise, all within the confines of a daily schedule of administrative chaos.

My experience as a dealer sales representative with manufacturer salespeople was enlightening. They consistently visited my branch and met with the manager. Some of them persuaded the manager to allow a ride along with me in the field. At first, I was flattered. Later I became annoyed. They spouted the same feature-benefit presentations that I learned on their factory tours, thus adding little to the dialogue. Worse yet, they spewed sales advice and presumed they were better salespeople than I was because they were "higher" in the supply chain. I finally told my manager that I refused to work with them anymore.

He assured me they thought I was a great sales partner. In return, I assured my manager that I believed him because I was the one generating all the energy and appointments. All they had to do was show up and blab about their product. The next time one of the reps asked about riding along, my manager told the sales rep to talk to me directly.

He was a rep for a popular skylight company. He told me that his skylights would probably not be a big part of my sales or even my customer's, but that the sale of a skylight could lead to the sale of other products. Then he shocked me by telling me about a contractor he wanted me to meet; he was giving me a lead! Predictably, the skylight salesman was one with whom I found great benefit of working cooperatively. I let the other salespeople at my branch know about him and facilitated introductions. In short, I became his advocate.

At first I was uncomfortable with his company's terminology. I didn't want to make a mistake. The rep made sure he was available to help while I placed my initial orders and literally sat with me as I filled out paperwork. Eventually I had complete confidence in his products, terminology, and ordering procedures. I also enjoyed the fact that the product was less price sensitive and provided an easy way for me to increase my sales margins, the basis of my compensation. One day he called and found out I had an order to place and offered his assistance. "I got this," I said with confidence. He thanked me for the order, which I placed unassisted.

That is how you build competent confidence.

Measuring Advocacy

The study of the learning process has concluded that people grow through a very consistent process while learning how to complete a task. The first stage is *unconscious incompetence* where the performer is unaware of the things they don't know; I didn't know skylights could be a good lead-in to the sale of my primary products. The second stage is *conscious incompetence*, where the performer knows they are unable to perform a task and are usually uncomfortable if expected to do so; I didn't know the skylight terminology or product line until the salesman educated me. These are the early learning stages of competence.

The stage of conscious incompetence is the emotional challenge to address and the key to building advocacy. It's already been established that the resellers are frequently working in a very complex environment where resistance to change is high. Conscious incompetence is more than a skill level; it's an emotional level of fear and anxiety.

With support that develops both competence and emotional security, the performer is able to complete a task with *conscious competence*. In the case of the skylights, I eventually learned the terminology and was willing to place an unassisted order because the coaching helped and elevated me to the level of *unconscious competence*. I had mastered the product line enough that I could comfortably promote the product, place orders on my own, and even assist my colleagues at the branch.

The measurement of confident competence comes not from the number of accounts a salesperson manages, but from the number of advocates within those accounts. In the modern era of CRM technology, it's a simple process of measurement. The initial measurement of advocacy, Level 1, is to assess the number of contacts in the salesperson's Rolodex or database. Level 2 engagement occurs when the salesperson can verify that the potential advocates have at least received an orientation to the product line. Level 3 occurs when the first order is successfully placed without incident. Level 4, the top level of advocacy, occurs when the salesperson for the reseller can be verified as a competent administrator of the product line without assistance and a proactive promoter of the brand.

The power of this model is that, like other aspects of behavioral sales economics, it lends itself well to the tested and observed theory that was introduced earlier. Presuming that a salesperson discovers the power of the advocacy model in individual circumstances, the opportunity to measure advocacy on a global scale as a macrosales economic metric is present. It is more than a theory; it's a proven practice that has been tested in a multitude of circumstances. The sales of wine, air conditioners, cooking knives, plumbing fixtures, and numerous other products have proven the success of the program.

Pop quiz! Which is more profitable and stable?

A. Eight dealers at which the sales representative has no contact with *their* salespeople, nor any clear evidence of frontline support for the program.

B. Eight committed sales advocates at two dealers that are verified sales contributors to the brand.

The answer should be obvious.

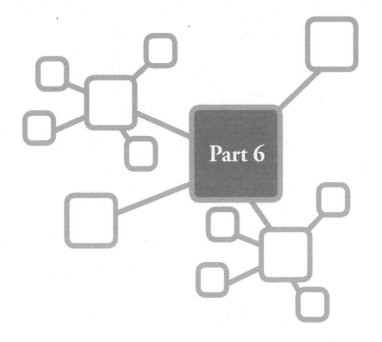

Part 6

AFTERWORD

19

The Power of Sales Science

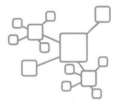

Telling Is Not Coaching

The adolescent baseball player looks adorable in his ill-fitting uniform as he walks to the plate while pictures are taken. The cute and lovable child we see playing an inconsequential game with other children sees himself as a warrior. He faces the challenge of a sphere being hurled in his direction. He must conquer his fears of being hit by the sphere and, moreover, strike it fiercely to prove his capabilities to the tribe. In his world, he is among peers trying to establish his credentials.

He strikes out. In a moment of frustration and anger, he argues with the umpire, throws his bat and helmet, swears about his misfortune, and returns to the bench where he stews. His frustrated manager approaches before asking and answering, "What is wrong with you? That is no way to behave." The budding young warrior receives the words and quiets, but is not calmed. He has not been prepared for the battle, but nonetheless was told *during* the performance to adhere to an expectation that was never established.

My business colleague Alswinn Kieboom, the parent to two major league baseball players and a fine athlete himself, shared a story of leadership success that he calls the difference between coaching and telling. "They will strike out," Kieboom assures them, "and are instructed during practices to turn without saying a word to the umpire, walk to the dugout, take the ten seconds to silently cope, and then it's over. It's time to refocus on the game and root for your teammates." In this way, he is *coaching* his players to deal with adversity *before* the heat of the moment. It is too late to *tell* the performer in the heat of battle. Telling is not coaching.

Sales coaching is the same...and different. Training, practice, and clear expectations are vital. Unlike sports and other endeavors, however, where the coach is forced to sit on the sidelines and observe, the sales coach can, and *must*, enter the field of play. Training can occur in the safe confines of the planning room where skills and confidence are produced, but it is not enough. In the field of play, particularly in the sales profession, the coach's role is to offer tailored performance feedback for each salesperson and sometimes includes a *demonstration of expected behaviors.*

The Sales Hero's Journey

Whether the coach observes from the sidelines or enters the battle, the legacy of learning must be passed on. We don't get practice rounds in selling. We can learn and practice situations in the classroom, but ultimately the sales calls that count *are* our practice rounds. This is where the salesperson needs guidance to become the *true* sales hero. An EMT technician can learn mouth-to-mouth resuscitation in the classroom, but needs the field guidance to of a veteran EMT in the heat of the moment for the final attainment of the skill or else people die. The ritual of coaching includes a demonstration of performance that is later practiced by the apprentice while receiving feedback from the mentor.

It is the ritual that has been mythologized for millennia. Joseph Campbell writes in *The Hero with a Thousand Faces*, "A hero ventures forth from the world of common day into a region of supernatural wonder: fabulous forces are there encountered and a decisive victory is won: the hero comes back from this mysterious adventure with the power to bestow boons on his fellow man." This is how skills and power are passed down and enhanced.

Campbell illustrated that the mythological path of the hero is consistent through time. It begins when the hero realizes he has a calling to answer and, at that exact moment, the mentor mystically appears—as in, *when the student is ready, the teacher appears*. The mentor shares secret powers with the young apprentice, a hero-in-the-making. The apprentice works to harness the power and encounters predictable difficulties along the way. Before he can manifest the power outwardly, he must face his demons and endure a transformation from within. This happens when the apprentice on his journey is introduced to the oracle, who is both a seer of the future and a shepherd on the hero's journey. Only after the hero sees the vision and harnesses the power from within will he emerge on the other side as the successful warrior leader.

In the confines of his little cave, the three-foot-high green oracle harnesses his mystical powers and lifts the immense and spaceship from the muck only to hear his apprentice warrior say, "I don't believe it."

"That is why you fail," says Yoda, the oracle with the secret to unlocking "the force." He must demonstrate for his apprentice that failure is part of the journey. He will strike out and must learn to cope with the failure in order to achieve success. It is part of the journey. This is the myth of the young hero, Skywalker. He must go into the cave and slice the head off the demon inside his own dreams, in the form of his father Darth Vader, before he can emerge a fully realized hero.

Not coincidentally, a young man named George Lucas studied with Joseph Campbell and modeled a popular movie on the mythological hero's journey. It is the story of the hero achieving the necessary power that is handed down for generations. "Prometheus ascended to the heavens, stole fire from the gods, and descended. Jason sailed through the Clashing Rocks into a sea of marvels, circumvented the dragon that guarded the Golden Fleece, and returned with the fleece and the power to wrest his rightful throne from a usurper." In modern Western culture, one of the most popular hero myths is the story of King Arthur.

It is his ability to pull the sword from the stone that unlocks the secret power. This is the power that enables him to attain his rightful throne and, moreover, share the power with the Knights of the Round Table. As the hero, Arthur, lies on his deathbed, the instructions are to cast the sword into the lake. There is debate about whether the power of the sword should be so hastily disposed. Of course the mortals receive the inevitable answer when the hand from the lady of the lake rises to catch the sword, symbolizing the protection of the power and a sign that it shall endure.

The salesman has been portrayed in modern mythology with negative and harshly judgmental archetypes. Movies, our modern tales of mythology, abound with stories of manipulative, selfish salespeople prepared to take money from innocent victims. David Mamet's *Glengarry Glen Ross* portrayed the clown, conniver, and beggar, all of them struggling with overcoming demons, albeit in this case to filch from their victims. Arthur Miller's *Death of a Salesman* illustrates the tragedy of the sales clown who wakes one day to realize a world has passed him by and the social connections that earned him his living are no longer available to protect him. Barry Levinson's *Tin Men* illustrates the legacy of the conniver systematically handed down from one salesman to the next. Hundreds more stories have portrayed negative sales archetypes.

The mythology manifests itself into reality by infiltrating the consciousness. Myths are not just stories we tell and hear; they reveal our collective psychology. The salesperson therefore becomes conflicted because the moral lessons from one set of myths conflict with the pressure for results *and* the nagging inner demons created by working in a profession mythologized as dishonorable. The replacement inner myth created by the salesperson to replace the clown and conniver is the false hero, a victim and beggar, advocating too strongly for the buyer. The real sales hero is the one building advocates for the cause of the tribe while still satisfying obligations to the buyer.

Selling is a noble profession when the power is harnessed and used properly. It is time to replace negative archetypes with the professional image of the warrior sales hero. Selling is a profession as old as humanity that began when tribes interacted to share food, technology, and practical goods like animal hides, arrow tips, and small pots. Selling is vital to the success of fair trade and should be embraced in that vein.

The Power Is Science

The profession, like all others, has evolved. The practices that once worked in medicine have been replaced with the modern tools of man's latest creations. The wheel has given way to the chariot, covered wagon, automobile, and eventually self-driving cars. Lore is passed down and improved with every generation. The selling techniques and tools of the past must give way to the skills and technology of the present.

Today's sales hero is the warrior who embraces science as the tool as powerful as Prometheus's fire, Jason's fleece, or Arthur's stone. The warrior acquires the power and then passes it on. This is the path of the warrior sales hero who will evolve to become the mentor for future warrior sales heroes. The power is not to be cast aside as Arthur mistakenly believed, but shared in the tradition of Prometheus, Jason, and Yoda.

Sales advocacy is leadership. The warrior sales leader creates advocacy with customers and employees. There is no difference in the performance with insiders (i.e., employees) and outsiders (i.e., customers) of the tribe. Their joint advocacy for the tribe are contingent on the credibility established by the warrior leader. Warrior leadership authority can only be established by credibility made by recruiting followers, not prisoners. Employees and clients must be inspired voluntarily to follow the warrior sales leader into battle. True leadership begins by *recruiting* the right apprentices, *communicating vision, coaching, monitoring performance,* and *releasing performers...* all performers. Yes, all performers. The successful warriors are released to fulfill their path within the tribe and mentor new recruits while the unsuccessful apprentices are released to find a better path for their destiny.

Advocacy is more than a sales model. It is the science of leadership. Trial, observation, and proactive consciousness are the scientific skills of behavioral sales economics that produce forward improvement through past experiences. The science of microsales provides the measurements to enhance sales calls and relationships. Macrosales science provides the numbers necessary to achieve audacious long-term goals with certainty.

I am not asking you to believe any concept shared in this body of work, but instead asking you to test the theories. Given the choice of believing everything you have read and not doing anything versus doubting the work in its entirety and testing the theories, I prefer you choose the latter. Leadership requires the power and willingness to let all sales actions stand up to the scrutiny of science. Sales economics provides the science of sales achievement and hopefully a little more. Perhaps the science will provide you success and confidence in life.

Bibliography

Campbell, Joseph. *The Hero with a Thousand Faces*. New York: Pantheon Books, 1949.

Case, Linda W. *The Remodeler's Guide to Making & Managing Money: A Common Sense Approach to Optimizing Compensation and Profit*. Silver Spring: Remodelers Advantage, Inc. 1996.

Cialdini, Robert B. *Influence: The Psychology of Persuasion*. New York: HarperCollins, 2006.

Collins, Jim. *Good to Great: Why Some Companies Make the Leap... and Others Don't*. New York: HarperCollins, 2001.

Collins, Jim and Morten T. Hansen. *Great by Choice: Uncertainty, Chaos, and Luck—Why Some Thrive Despite Them All*. New York: HarperCollins, 2011.

Ericsson, Anders and Robert Pool. *Peak: Secrets from the New Science of Expertise*. New York: Houghton Mifflin Harcourt, 2016.

Gladwell, Malcolm. *Blink: The Power of Thinking without Thinking*. New York: Little, Brown and Company, 2005.

Gladwell, Malcolm. *Outliers: The Story of Success*. New York: Little, Brown and Company, 2008.

Harris, Thomas A. *I'm OK—You're OK*. New York: Harper & Row, 1969.

James, Bill. *Baseball Abstract*. New York: Villard Books, 1985.

Kahneman, Daniel. *Thinking Fast and Slow*. New York: Farrar, Straus and Giroux, 2011.

Lewis, Michael: *Money Ball: The Art of Wining and Unfair Game*. New York: W.W. Norton & Company, 2003.

Lewis, Michael: *The Undoing Project: A Friendship That Changed Our Minds*. New York: W.W. Norton & Company, 2017.

Levitt, Steven D. and Stephen J. Dubner. *Freakonomics: A Rogue Economist Explores the Hidden Side of Everything*. New York: HarperCollins, 2005.

Mackay, Harvey B. *Swim with the Sharks Without Being Eaten Alive: Outsell, Outmanage, Outmotivate, and Outnegotiate Your Competition*. New York: HarperCollins, 1988.

Thaler, Richard H. *Misbehaving: The Making of Behavioral Economics*. New York: W. W. Norton & Company, 2016.

About the Author

RICK DAVIS is a sought after speaker, trainer, sales consultant, and the president of Building Leaders, Inc. He is the author of *The Sales Secret* and a world-class magazine columnist who has been awarded gold and silver medals from the American Society of Business Publishing Editors. Rick's earned his BA in economics while also studying mathematics, computers and acting at the University of Michigan. He resides in Chicago, Illinois, where he continues to be a curious student of many subjects, all of which he uses to produce universal messages that resonate with his audiences.

During a thirty year career, he has delivered keynote presentations and training to tens of thousands of people at companies large and small…but mostly medium. For more information on keynotes, training, or Building Leaders online learning platform, visit **www.buildingleaders.com**.

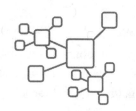